THE WONDER OF TRUST

THE WONDER OF TRUST

Time Tested Processes
To Encourage
Business Owners To Live
Out A Life Of Significance,
Impacting The Kingdom

BILL BOESTERD

THE WONDER OF TRUST

ISBN-13: 978-1537237688

ISBN-10: 1537237683

Copyright © 2016 by Bill Boesterd

Create Space Independent Publishing Platform

All rights reserved solely by the author. No part of this book may be reproduced, stored in a retrieval system or transmitted by any means without the written permission of the author.

All Scriptures quoted are from the NIV (New International Version), unless otherwise stated.

DEDICATION

This book is dedicated to my wife Joanne, who has faithfully stood by my side throughout our years in business.

Joanne, I could not have succeeded without you. Your continuous trust and support and unfailing love provided the fuel to continue.

CONTENTS

Acknowledgement ix

Prologue: Setting The Pace xi

Introduction: The Starting Point 1

1– Knowing And Appreciating Your Limitations 13

2– Knowing Who You Are And Where You Are Going 23

3– Acknowledging Others Ability To Contribute To The Building of Your Team 35

4– Trusting And Respecting Others 45

5– Clearing The Chaos: Organizing To Clarity 51

6– Hiring Strategically 61

7– Organizing Further to Reduce and Hopefully Eliminate Unneeded Challenges 67

8– Understanding Effective Delegation 75

9– Stop Assuming. Start Inspecting What You Expect 85

10– Do Not Guess. Start Accounting For It 91

11– Stop Working Overtime. Start Having
      Some Fun 101

12– Start Working "On" Your Business 107

13– Doing Business From A Kingdom
      Perspective 115

Epilogue 129

References 131

ACKNOWLEDGEMENT

To Raymond Aaron and your 10-10-10 book writing program, without which I would likely never have begun. Your belief in others, and in me, lit a spark to do what I did: write a book.

To my children, thank you for encouraging me to complete this writing project. Your encouragement, love, and support mean more than you know. You are a blessing to me.

To all the wonderful people that contributed to Denbow's success over its lifetime, thank you for your energy, encouragement, and faithfulness to our mission that has allowed us to survive, thrive, and make a difference for many.

To you who have taken on various leadership responsibilities over the years within Denbow; Mrs. Green's Landscape Centre, Superior Stone Slinger Services, Clear Creek Broilers and the other business opportunities I have engaged in, thank you so much. You embraced the trust given you, and you gave back more than what was expected. You gave me the freedom to enjoy the richest of business experiences, and the people that came with it.

To my editor, Cleveland O. McLeish, thank you for taking this project on, keeping me motivated and moving forward and then putting the final touches on it to turn it into a book. I couldn't have done it without you.

To Andrew & Jackie Stam, I extend my deep appreciation and gratitude for the trust they extended to me at the age of 25 to take on and continue the business they had started. Now over 35 years later, we continue to grow and enjoy this opportunity.

Finally, I want to thank everyone who contributed small or great to this vision; Jerome Bates, for your ongoing encouragement, my daughter Michelle for checking in and keeping me moving forward, my son Cody, for insisting you are looking forward to the first signed copy, Uncle Bob for repeatedly asking with encouragement when it was going to be done.

To Gary Teichrob for your story, Jack Hoogendoorn for your story and faithful example, Peter VanGiesen for your mentorship, and so many more that encouraged me along this journey of life in business. I am so grateful to all of you.

PROLOGUE
Setting The Pace

The day had arrived. A sizable group of employees and friends shared memories, shed tears, shook hands, and offered hugs as Gary Teichrob, founder and part owner of Tycrop Manufacturing in Chilliwack BC, wound up his last day at work. He was retiring. Although his emotionally torn employees agreed they would miss him, they also agreed if one had to earn the right to retire early, Gary at 47 years old certainly had. He had worked long and hard.

It had been a long haul, and with the challenges all business owners face day after day, after 27 years in business, Gary said, *"I was tired, ready for a break and keen to pursue new projects and ideas. I also had a business partner who was eager for the opportunity to take the reins and run the business."*

For the first year of his retirement, Gary said: *"I spent my time pursuing other interests, whether it was auto racing, traveling, or taking road trips on my Harley."* Enjoying his recreational hobbies and spending more time with family was initially a dream come true. However, two years into his retirement Gary found he was taking more of an interest, from a distance, in the business he had founded and fortunately, had retained shares in. The retirement dream was beginning to lack its former luster and the desire to engage more purposefully in what he understood most, business, was regaining his interest.

A few months' later, circumstances came about that called Gary back to the same business he had left behind, and he was ready. Today, almost ten years later, along with his business partners and a great team of people, each with individual strengths, they are driving the business forward together.

So, what's changed? The people he is surrounded by, sharing the challenges of business, and his restored energy. Gary says, "I came to the realization that the thrill of business excited me more than retirement."

Today we find Gary engaged in the areas of the business he enjoys, enthusiastically mentoring his team, and where time allows, other individuals on a similar journey. Gary is living out a life of significance. Gary's interest in retiring has completely vanished.

So, What About You?

Are you thinking of retiring? You are getting emails from business evaluators, wealth management consultants, financial planners, and more, all offering to help you plan your retirement years. You may be wondering how to make the best use of those years; travel, recreation, investing the net proceeds of your business sale. So many questions. So many choices. So many considerations.

Maybe, with the recent difficult years of business, a sale and retirement don't look as ideal as you'd like it to look. You have had financial setbacks, some difficult years, and yet you are tired. It has been a long road. The options for retirement are fewer than you had hoped for some years ago.

Whatever your reality, I am asking you today, is retirement or a business sale the only option? Why not consider a different option? Maybe your best years lie ahead of you, taking the experiences you have had in business; the setbacks, the failures, the wins, all those years now possibly giving you an opportunity to invest in others' that which you learned the hard way. You may have gone from success to significance, whatever your success may have been and is today. I am suggesting that you stay engaged in your business where you have an opportunity to enrich the lives of others for their benefit, and yours and most importantly, for the Kingdom.

Our society is in need of experienced leaders willing to mentor the next generation.

THE WONDER OF TRUST

I am writing you from my experience. It happened somewhat by accident or at least without intention initially. We were and are still a small company. It was around the year 2005, and British Columbia was awarded the 2010 winter Olympics. Our company works with forest residuals, taking the leftovers of a tree and turning it into something more valuable. At that time, we were offering an off-site in vessel composting service, taking what was usually burnt after an area of forest had been cleared and through that composting process turning it into a valuable product for reestablishing vegetation. 2010 Olympic contractors heard about our services and with a lot of the work in and around the village of Whistler British Columbia the concept of producing a valuable material that could be used to establish vegetation in the cleared areas to serve the Olympic venues, rather than burning the material, attracted their attention.

After a series of meetings, we were awarded a contract. This was great news for us. However, we knew it would also be one of the largest challenges that we had ever faced. We then realized with the extra manpower needed for this opportunity; we were in need of further organization within our company. It was this process of working together for weeks and then months that a small team of six people, including myself, was unintentionally formed. As we worked together to try and understand how we would be best organized to serve our existing clients and this new opportunity, I began to realize the benefit of working as a team. For the first time in my business life, I started to consider making decisions as a team, **by consensus, rather than on my own.**

I was challenged at first by this idea of giving up the privilege of making decisions on my own. Up until this time I had made most decisions on my own. Hiring and releasing of staff, purchase of equipment, policies and procedures, and much more. I was now suggesting to myself that if I were to responsibly and respectfully engage the team to make decisions with me, I would have no choice but to release many of those decisions I have made by myself in the past, to be made by consensus. After spending considerable time evaluating the pros and cons of this change, *I began to realize that there was much more opportunity available for me, for our team and our company to be experienced by the proposed changes.*

Now over ten years later I would not want to do it any other way. I will admit that there were times that I was quietly frustrated by not being able to make a decision on my own, but the benefits that we have enjoyed through working, thinking, strategizing, envisioning the future, and making strategic decisions together, far outweigh the few times that I have been frustrated.

Today, I am also at that age where many would consider the sale of their business or some way to release themselves from the responsibilities attached to business ownership or simply put, to retire. I can enthusiastically tell you that I have no such desire. I have every reason to stay engaged. I have an opportunity to mentor and coach our existing team. I have the opportunity to be involved in discovering ways in which we can add value to every member of our small business and beyond, while enjoying the freedom to travel, enjoy recreational opportunities and still have a privileged responsibility within our company and, my investment within the enterprise continues to grow.

> *"Never be so foolish as not to surround yourself with people smarter than yourself."*
> –Andrew Carnegie

In the quote above, Andrew Carnegie, the wealthy industrialist, shared with us one of his reasons for success.

I took careful note of this wise instruction for most of my years in business. I relied heavily on skills of others that surpassed my own. What I had not realized was the synergy available when these people were assembled into a purposeful team. Admittedly building a strong executive team is not something one should do in a hurry or without careful considerations. All this takes time.

Where Do You Start?

One practice I strongly advise is to understand the personality strengths ideally of all your employees and especially those you may consider engaging as a member of your executive team. There are some of these indicator tools on the market today. We have for quite some years now enjoyed the PSI (Personality Style Indicator) provided by CRG, the Consulting Resource Group in British Columbia. This tool and others help us to discern the strengths that our employees bring to our company. It also becomes easier to determine the missing strengths needed on a team.

Trust In The Ability Of Your Team

Another essential characteristic, which you the owner need to bring to the team, is the willingness to trust your team to perform to the best of their abilities. You need to be willing to let go and to believe in each member of your team. That belief in them needs to be displayed by you by stepping back where you can, as often as you can, and withholding that strong desire just to step in and decide on something that is taking some time to think through.

By intentionally resisting stepping in, your team grows to be more and more able to make the right decisions in your absence, and that is what you are looking for. You are seeking to build this team to think like you, value what you value, to act and decide like you would. The shaping of the culture of your company is very much your responsibility, and it is very likely that you have engaged in that responsibility for some years. Those values need to be embraced by your team so that in your absence your clients and your employees are treated and respected as if you were there.

The vision, mission, and values, which you feel strongly about, need to be articulated in writing. When these are clearly articulated, understood, and agree to by your executive team and referred to, as well as practiced, on a daily basis, *you will begin to enjoy the flexibility that you are looking for as an owner of your business.* I believe through my experience that when you get there, the sale of your business and retirement will not be so attractive.

Implementing And Training In The Standards Of Conduct

Another critical part of having a healthy executive team that leads by example and is respected by all members of the company are the standards of conduct. Standards such as respecting one another, being honest with one another, willing to be held accountable, extending trust, while having fun.

Organizational Chart

Having a clearly understood structure of responsibility is also vitally important. People need to know who to turn to, and for what. With a lack of clarity in this area, chaos is a likely companion. That is to be avoided at all costs. There are numerous ways to organize, and it will vary from one business to another. The key is to have clarity as your goal. Everyone in your organization should be clear as to who is responsible for what.

Policies And Procedures Need To Be Written Out

These are the foundational stones for how we do business here. The written policies and procedures articulate and define the culture of your business.

We have an employee handbook that answers almost every question a new or existing employee may ask, avoiding the heartaches that can result where the staff is unsure and decide on their own how something should be done or handled.

You might be asking what your role might be once you have brought your business to where it almost runs without you. One suggestion would be to enjoy a season of emotional refreshment. Take the time to be restored emotionally. Invest time in areas you may not have had the time for before; time with family and friends you may have been too busy for.

From Success To Significance

Living out a life of significance is where you have the opportunity to give back, to add value to others. This can be done through mentoring your team, and also making yourself available to mentor others. Our society is in need of good leaders who are willing to mentor other *'leaders in the making'*. **This could be the most rewarding season of your life.**

The Kingdom Perspective

The only real challenge I had with writing this book, is adding a more kingdom perspective to the concepts shared. I wanted this book to be relevant in this kingdom age that we are now living in. The church should not be equal to the world in how we live, and the decisions we make, as it relates to business. Our perspective should be higher, and more defined by eternal truth. It is for the glory of God, that we entered into business, to utilize the talents and gifts that He has deposited in us by His Holy Spirit. We know we will one day have to give an account concerning how we have used what we have been given. We are called to be good stewards of His blessings.

Prologue

So, business for us is more than just making money. It is rooted in a desire to make a lasting impact on the world for God and leave a good inheritance for our children's children. After all, that is what a good business person should do.

I encourage you to join us in this enriched business experience, to see how we can efficiently impact the Kingdom of God through business.

Enjoy the journey.

Bill Boesterd

Introduction
The Starting Point

I was about four years old when I decided what I wanted to do for the rest of my working life. I wanted to be a truck driver. Initially, this was due to the adventurous spirit of one of my uncles who introduced me to the truck driving profession by taking me on a ride-along. Unfortunately, when I decided I wanted to be a truck driver I also decided I did not need higher education. It was my father's relentless insistence that I complete at least the twelfth grade, which allowed me to graduate from high school. However, I did not put my best effort into school, and as a result, I barely completed the twelfth grade, graduating with average grades. Had I realize at that time that my life would be engaged in more than operating a truck; I would have reconsidered my approach to education. Fortunately, God can use us just as we are in building His kingdom and He can make us great despite our limitations if we seek Him and have faith.

I take this opportunity to encourage those who may read this while they are getting an education that no matter what or where you wish to be employed or engaged in life, be sure to pursue higher education to enable you to achieve more. I have often encouraged young people undecided about their future career and educational goals to consider pursuing a business degree, as there is a business side to everything. With a degree in business, you can still pursue a hands-on career. If the opportunity comes along and the desire is there, you have the education to take you further than you would without it. In whatever we do, education is necessary, whether we require it for business, our personal lives or our spiritual growth. We must become willing disciples to obtain knowledge.

I am also giving a word of encouragement to those who feel they lack the education to pursue the challenge of taking their business to a higher level. As you could discover it is possible, without traditional education, to still take your business to places you never dreamed or imagined possible. But we must put God first in everything we do. Everything is achievable with God, who has given us everything we need to follow our goals and dreams.

It is good to remember that Kingdom living is all about claiming the fruits that God has stored up for us by having faith, pursuing our dreams and allowing Him to manifest everything for us. Mathew 6: 33 says, **"But seek first his kingdom and his righteousness, and all these things will be given to you as well."** It is my experience that without faith in the Eternal One nothing can be achieved, and anything achieved does not bring lasting success and happiness.

Introduction - The Starting Point

As we become educated in business, so must we become educated in all that pertains to the Kingdom of God. In fact, the same qualities that we seek to exemplify when we live a God-filled life are the same qualities that will also make us succeed in business. These qualities are called the fruits of the spirit. They are love, joy, peace, patience, kindness, goodness, faithfulness, gentleness, and self-control. These are keys to building successful relationships and to building a successful business, and these are the spiritual fruits that those who believe that God's Kingdom is here and now should embody if we are to be the beacon of light for those who do not know Christ.

St. Mathew 16: 24-26, Then Jesus said to his disciples, "Whoever wants to be my disciple must deny themselves and take up their cross and follow me. For whoever wants to save their life will lose it, but whoever loses their life for me will find it. What good will it be for someone to gain the whole world, yet forfeit their soul? Or what can anyone give in exchange for their soul?

In all things, we must remember that the greatest profit we can gain as children of God is our salvation and the salvation of others. By us modeling Christ many will come to know of His wonder and come to glorify the Eternal Father.

This book is written primarily to encourage any business owner who may have thought they did not have it in them to achieve some of the dreams and goals they have. As you will soon discover, almost anything is possible if you have faith in the Eternal Father and if you leave behind a few of the hindrances and stumbling blocks that may hold you back. One of those stumbling blocks could be a lack of faith in the great I Am or a lack of confidence in yourself or maybe a level of pride that is disallowing you to trust others with some of the responsibilities you have kept for yourself.

Another hindrance may be others telling you that you do not have it in you, you do not have the needed education, you do not have the experience, and that you should just be satisfied with where you are. Truthfully, there may be a host of other hindrances holding you back. I hope by reading these few chapters, you will discover that you do have an opportunity to take your business to places you have never dreamed possible and that everything is possible with the One who created us.

I want to enlighten you on some steps you can take to enjoy your business and your life, but not necessarily the details of how to do it. It is my objective to open up your understanding to the steps and procedures I took to enjoy this journey. I encourage you to consider the same, to enjoy the rest of your life and business. I also want to add that this was my experience in business and these are the steps that I took to get to a place in life and business where I thoroughly enjoy both. I am confident that the steps my wife and I have taken in our businesses have allowed key people on our teams to feel valued and appreciated and to enjoy the challenges that accompany their responsibilities.

By facilitating others to achieving their true potentials, we are following the steps of Christ because we know that what the Father truly desires for us, His children, is a fulfilled life. Following the steps of Christ means embodying His goodness. To impact the Kingdom through business, internal and external customers and clients must see a difference in how the children of God operate to come to want to know God for themselves.

It is important that you take the time to understand yourself. What do you want for yourself and your family or for those that are engaged with you in the business? Some go into business to be self-employed and thereby not having to take directives from another. To enjoy the flexibility and the responsibility of deciding what will be done on a given day is of great satisfaction and is very important for some. They want flexibility, and they want to decide for themselves what and how they will engage in the business. They are self-employed. For some, that is very satisfying. There was a period where that is all I wanted. I wanted to own one truck and had no further ambition than being able to make some decisions for myself.

Successive Planning

It is said that one way to decide whether someone has a successful business, is to walk away from it for one year. When you return, the business should be the same or greater than when you left. If that is not the case and the company can hardly do without you, the business more than likely has you as an employee. Again, it is different for everyone and the question need to be asked what level of responsibility do you want to take on?

In determining what we want for ourselves, we must understand what is our purpose as children living in the Kingdom of God. The whole purpose is to be able to walk in the steps of Christ. Jesus taught His disciples to continue the Father's work long after He would be gone. So successive planning is part of business and part of being a child of God. We must want to raise others up. To watch others grow to the stage where they can assume new responsibilities is a beautiful thing.

I agree with other leaders that one of the responsibilities of business owners is to grow the abilities of others. As business owners, in particular for those embodying the principles of Kingdom living, those who have come into our area of influence, should they leave at some time, should leave with more capacity and more ability than when they first arrived. As Christians, we are called to emulate Christ in everything we do. The opportunity to grow our business and assist others to grow should be one of our focuses. That is why my desire is to be a business owner involved in the coaching and mentoring of others, allowing them to grow in their opportunity to manage and lead. They, in turn, will hopefully focus on developing those they are called to supervise and lead daily, and the link in the chain will keep growing and growing like the little mustard seed in Jesus's parable. In Matthew 13:31-32 Jesus said, **"The kingdom of heaven is like a mustard seed, which a man took and planted in his field. Though it is the smallest of all seeds, yet when it grows, it is the largest of garden plants and becomes a tree, so that the birds come and perch in its branches."**

When you have built a team of the right people around you, you should be able to walk away from your business for a lengthy period, and the business should continue to grow with little direction from you. This is you demonstrating trust.

My journey of trust started early in life. One clear memory I have is when I was twelve years old. I grew up around trucks and equipment. My father was employed at a Ready Mix Concrete Operation. The Plant was situated alongside a river. When the river was low enough, gravel was extracted from the river gravel bars. This served two purposes; aggregates for concrete batching and to allow the river to flow freely during spring snow melts, resulting in high river runoff. One fall Saturday I was asked if I could drive a gravel truck out to the river bar. Cor, one of the plant subcontractors, would take his loader off the river bar at night and bring it back in the morning. He would walk back to get his truck. This particular morning, he was a bit behind and to catch up on some lost time, he asked me if I could drive his gravel truck to the river bar while he drove the loader. He would be right ahead of me in his loader. Cor respectfully asked my dad if this would be okay. My father approved and off we went. I was twelve years old, carefully driving a tandem axle gravel truck. I felt like I grew a few years that morning. What an accomplishment to be trusted to drive this vehicle.

The journey of trust is when a person speaks into the life of another saying *'I trust you to take on this mission.'* When that conversation happens, the person spoken to grows in their capacity to take on a new challenge. The wonder of trust is often wonderfully displayed by many parents as they encourage a timid child, *"You can do it. I believe in you. I trust you to take on this challenge"*.

The greatest Being we can bestow trust in is God. **Trust in the Lord with all your heart and lean not on your own understanding; in all your ways submit to him, and he will make your paths straight. (Proverbs 3:5-6).** Trust is a wonder. Our Creator trusts us to dictate our lives and we are free in His kingdom to err and learn.

Introduction - The Starting Point

What we do with that trust is up to us. Where we fall, He is there to pick us up as our friend, confidant, assistance and comforter. It is like the parable of the talents.

"Again, it will be like a man going on a journey, who called his servants and entrusted his wealth to them. To one he gave five bags of gold, to another two bags, and to another one bag, each according to his ability. Then he went on his journey. The man who had received five bags of gold went at once and put his money to work and gained five bags more. So also, the one with two bags of gold gained two more. But the man who had received one bag went off, dug a hole in the ground and hid his master's money. "After a long time the master of those servants returned and settled accounts with them. The man who had received five bags of gold brought the other five. 'Master,' he said, 'you entrusted me with five bags of gold. See, I have gained five more.' "His master replied, 'Well done, good and faithful servant! You have been faithful with a few things; I will put you in charge of many things. Come and share your master's happiness!' "The man with two bags of gold also came. 'Master,' he said, 'you entrusted me with two bags of gold; see, I have gained two more.' "His master replied, 'Well done, good and faithful servant! You have been faithful with a few things; I will put you in charge of many things. Come and share your master's happiness!' "Then the man who had received one bag of gold came. 'Master,' he

said, 'I knew that you are a hard man, harvesting where you have not sown and gathering where you have not scattered seed. So I was afraid and went out and hid your gold in the ground. See, here is what belongs to you.' "His master replied, 'You wicked, lazy servant! So you knew that I harvest where I have not sown and gather where I have not scattered seed? Well then, you should have put my money on deposit with the bankers, so that when I returned I would have received it back with interest. "'So take the bag of gold from him and give it to the one who has ten bags. For whoever has will be given more, and they will have an abundance. Whoever does not have, even what they have will be taken from them. And throw that worthless servant outside, into the darkness, where there will be weeping and gnashing of teeth.' (St. Matthew 25:14-30)

We must not be like the servant who buries his talent; we must grow our talent.

Trust is a beautiful thing. A good portion of the relationship between Jesus and us as disciples is based on trust. First Jesus taught His disciples and then trusted them to continue His work. It was upon the understanding or revelation that Peter 'The Rock' received that He built His church. We are children of the Kingdom of God, and if we intend for His kingdom to come or if we believe that His Kingdom has come, we must live as we would in His

Kingdom. Remember, faith is the evidence of things not seen. We will be rewarded when we give others trust.

A good part of this book is written based on the wonder of trust. An excellent transition happens when someone entrusts something to another.

1
Knowing And Appreciating Your Limitations

Philippians 4:19
And my God will meet all your needs according to the riches of his glory in Christ Jesus.

It was 1998, and Peter Van Giesen joined our company as Vice President of Operations. This decision was the result of a few realities we were experiencing. I was actively involved on two national boards that took me away from our business a few days at a time throughout the year. Our business was growing. We were operating four different business services under one banner, as well as a landscape supply business, and a broiler chicken farm. To develop these opportunities effectively, I needed business experience and expertise I did not have. What were my options? I could make do with what little business experience I had, and as John Maxwell says, bump up to the level of my business leadership lid, or I could admit my lack of needed understanding and experience, and surround myself with people smarter than myself in areas of need that I did not master. I chose the latter, and I am glad I did. I have had an incredible business experience, thanks to people whom I entrusted to carry out what they were good at, and they, in turn, trusted me to treat them with respect.

It was during this time that I enrolled myself in the Simon Fraser University course of study called the Executive Management Development Program. The program focused on seven key areas of management. This is one program I have always appreciated. It allowed me to discover the areas of business acumen that I fell short of with my lack of business education. This course of study did not make me an expert, but it did open my understanding to the vital needs of a successful growing business.

There were some fundamental discoveries, procedural upgrades, processes, and tools we introduced during Peter's tenure with Denbow. It was a time of organizational development that I enjoyed immensely; the fruit of which we still enjoy today.

I learned about mystery shopping, customer satisfaction research, PSI, among many other opportunities. We developed an employee handbook, a safety program, and a higher level of in-house financial accountability and reporting. We will talk about these in a later chapter.

Knowing And Appreciating Your Limitations

While I strongly encourage bringing others around us where we fall short, I want to help you understand that you bring more to your business opportunity than you may have realized. Very often we compare ourselves to others. We can lack confidence, and our business growth is stunted for fear that we do not have what it takes to take it to the next level. I am convinced that you have more ability than you realize. I found this to be true about me, and everyone we have worked with.

Where you lack faith in yourself and others, put it in God. Philippians 4:6-7 says, **"Do not be anxious about anything, but in every situation, by prayer and petition, with thanksgiving, present your requests to God. And the peace of God, which transcends all understanding, will guard your hearts and your minds in Christ Jesus."** Do not get anxious about letting others take the lead. If you've done your due diligence and there is nothing to fear, send God your prayers and supplications about whatever may concern you, have faith and watch your business grow. You have an opportunity to be an effective team leader when others are assigned roles that fit them.

I borrowed a few thoughts from Napoleon Hill's book ***'Think and Grow Rich'*** that helped me understand that I brought more to the table than I had realized. If your business is now at a point where you are feeling overrun with responsibilities, and opportunities continue to come, and your business continues to grow, you very likely have what it takes to take your business to the next level. Take a look at what Napoleon Hill discovered in his interview with Henry Ford many years ago.

Napoleon Hill in his book 'Think and Grow Rich' describes an educated man as follows:

'An educated man is not necessarily one who has an abundance of general or specialized knowledge. An educated man is one who has so developed the faculties of his mind that he may acquire anything he wants, or its equivalent, without violating the rights of others." Ford comes well within the meaning of this definition.

During the world war, a Chicago newspaper published certain editorials in which, among other statements, Henry Ford was called "an ignorant pacifist." Mr. Ford objected to the statements, and brought suit against the paper for libeling him. The suit was tried in the courts. The attorneys for the paper pleaded justification, and placed Mr. Ford, himself, on the witness stand, for the purpose of proving to the jury that he was ignorant. The attorneys asked Mr. Ford a variety of questions; all of them intended to prove, by his own evidence, that, while he might possess considerable specialized knowledge pertaining to the manufacture of automobiles, he was mainly ignorant.

Mr. Ford was plied with such questions as the following: "Who is Benedict Arnold?" And "How many soldiers did the British send over to America to put down the rebellion of 1776?" In answer to the last question, Mr. Ford replied, "I do not know the exact number of soldiers the British sent over, but I have heard that it was superbly a larger number than ever went back."

Finally Mr. Ford became tired of this line of questioning, and replying to a particularly offensive question, he leaned over, pointed his finger at the lawyer who had asked the question and said "If I should really want to answer the foolish question you have just asked, or any of the other questions you have been asking me, let me remind you that I have a row of electric push-buttons on my desk, and by pushing the right button, I can summon to me a man who can answer any question I desire to ask concerning the business to which I am devoting most of my efforts. Now will you kindly tell me, why should I clutter up my mind with general knowledge for the purpose of being able to answer such questions, when I have people around me who can supply any knowledge I require?" There certainly was good logic to that reply.

That answer floored the lawyer. Every person in the courtroom realized it was the answer, not of an ignorant man, but of a man of education. Any man is educated who knows where to get knowledge when he needs it, and how to organize that knowledge into definite plans. Through the assistance of his "mastermind" group, Henry Ford had at his command all the specialized knowledge he needed to enable him to become one of the wealthiest men in America.

It is not essential that he have this in his own mind. Surely no person who has sufficient inclination and intelligence to read a book of this nature possibly missed the significance of this illustration.[1]

What Henry Ford described to his audience and the court that day was that he had come to understand how to assemble information, retrieve knowledge, and in the process honor others by surrounding himself with people that were smarter than himself in their areas of expertise. Because he trusted, encouraged, respected, honored, and appreciated these team members, they, in turn, shared with him his need for information and specific knowledge in areas that he was not well informed.

Andrew Carnegie, a wealthy industrialist, was quoted as saying *"Never be so foolish as not to surround yourself with people that are smarter than yourself."* I use this quote often.

It is possible that in many areas of business you do not have the skills or training needed to take your business to the next level on your own. For you to go and receive an education in all these areas of need to take the business to the next level would possibly take years. However, there

---

[1] McCreadie, Karen, and Napoleon Hill. Napoleon Hill's Think and Grow Rich a 52 Brilliant Ideas Interpretation. Oxford: Infinite Ideas, 2008.

are people already trained that are more than willing to join your team or you probably already have them within your company. If not, they are likely available to join you, and you can form a team that strives for excellence.

As disciples, we must be cognizant that we have a lot to learn from others. Just as it is vital in business that we recognize the greater ability of others, we must acknowledge in our everyday lives the invaluable contribution of others. We must also understand that the Eternal Father will supply all our needs, and when that person comes along to take us higher than we have ever been, it is God who has brought us what we have been praying for. But when we fail to recognize the ability of others, we turn our gifts away.

No man or woman can be an island. We were birthed here on Earth, one of Gods uncountable planets, with billions of other persons. We are meant to function in groups and the Kingdom of God, all the stars are allowed to shine. Therefore, we must recognize and foster the abilities of those amongst us. In doing so, we have an opportunity also to grow to heights of leadership we never imagined.

Recognizing that another person's ability in something is greater than ours requires humility. We are called to humble ourselves before others. Humility is not only an endearing quality; it also allows us to learn from others.

What does it cost to admit that we do not know something and that we need help?

Humility is a quality that Christians should strive for. It sets us apart from the rest of the business community. What we want to be is different; so, our light can shine, and others may see it and come to know our Father and join us in building His Kingdom here on earth. 1 Peter 5:5-6 says, '**In the same way, you who are younger, submit yourselves to your elders. All of you, clothe yourselves with humility toward one another, because, "God opposes the proud but shows favor to the humble." Humble yourselves, therefore, under God's mighty hand, that he may lift you up in due time.**' Proverbs 22:4 also says, **"Humility is the fear of the Lord; its wages are riches and honor and life."**

When you invite people to come around you that have a skill or understanding that would add a measure of excellence to your management team, to lend and share their understanding, you honor them for the training and experience they have amassed both through education and experience. At the same time, your team becomes stronger. Never be so foolish not to surround yourself with people that are smarter and wiser than you are. Do not allow pride to get in your way.

Admittedly it takes a level of humility to confess that one is not as particularly skilled or aware in an area as what might be needed. There is something to be said for the one that does have the humility, personality, and understanding to assemble a team around herself or himself, and thereby have this at their disposal. Everybody benefits from the team growing stronger, and as the company grows, more people have opportunities that they have not had in the past and clients are served at a level they have not experienced before. Everyone wins.

You very likely have a good understanding of the possibilities of what your business is capable of doing if given a chance. The only way that those dreams can be fulfilled is by assembling a team of people that carry the variety of experiences and skill sets needed. Yours is the opportunity to be the conductor of an orchestra, where within the orchestra there is a broad range of talented professionals. Without the understanding, the vision, and the ability of the conductor to assemble all those professionals and to draw from their wells of talent and experience resulting in rich melodic satisfying sound, the audience will be deprived of the deeply satisfying result. You are the conductor of your business. Realize the potential and engage it.

There is biblical justification for growing our teams. Solomon's wisdom is vital today. He says, **'Two are better than one, because they have a good return for their labor: If either of them falls down, one can help the other up. But pity anyone who falls and has no one**

to help them up. Also, if two lie down together, they will keep warm. But how can one keep warm alone? Though one may be overpowered, two can defend themselves. A cord of three strands is not quickly broken.' (Ecclesiastes 4:9-12). Solomon was describing the strength in numbers. When strands of cords become banded together like a rope, they are hard to break, but by themselves, they are like threads to be broken. There is strength in numbers. In life, it is the same as in business. We build relationships in Christ to form His Church. Together as one accord, we represent the unity that Jesus demonstrated on earth.

2
Knowing Who You Are And Where You Are Going

Genesis 12:1-3
The Lord had said to Abram, "Go from your country, your people and your father's household to the land I will show you. "I will make you into a great nation, and I will bless you; I will make your name great, and you will be a blessing. I will bless those who bless you, and whoever curses you I will curse; and all peoples on earth will be blessed through you."

Understanding who we are and the direction we intend to go is vital in our Christian walk and business. To understand others we must first understand ourselves. There are many personality tools that will help you understand your personality type. *The Personality Style Indicator* or PSI is an excellent way to understand your strengths. If you know your strengths, it is easier to assess the voids in your business and to see the opportunities that exist to build a strong team. Once you know your personality strengths, and you start to realize where you best fit, you can then start to look for other team members that complement the makeup of a complete team.

If we do not understand style, we may put people in positions they ought not to be in, and the individual is not able to excel and thus is not acknowledged for what he or she does best. The company can suffer because of inefficient operations, and an overall ineffective environment is experienced. For the company to operate as a smoothly working machine, we need to put people in the right positions of responsibility. The old saying of *'Round pegs in round holes'* makes a lot of sense in this case. Trying to drive a square peg into a round hole is a frustrating experience for the employee, the team and for you as a business owner. I have worked with Consulting Resource Group and have found their assessment tools to be very effective. There is a booklet form and a very comprehensive online form.

Paul says, **"For just as each of us has one body with many members, and these members do not all have the same function, so in Christ we, though many, form one body, and each member belongs to all the others. We have different gifts, according to the grace given to each of us. If your gift is prophesying, then prophesy in accordance with your faith." (Romans 12:4-6)**

Just as the church is one body in Christ with many different members with many different gifts and talents, we must strive to embody this unity in every relationship we build. All the gifts of personalities and talents belong to God and are for the building of His Kingdom.

The real aim is always to use the God given gifts of others for the betterment of His Kingdom, and this comes from us recognizing that we all are unique and have a unique role to play.

Our personality is an interesting and unique part of us. As I was growing up, I wanted to be a truck driver and nothing but a truck driver. Eventually, I became a truck driver. And at that time if somebody asked me one of the first things I probably said is that I was a truck driver. However, a truck driver was what I did, not who I was or who I am. I am a person that has a strength in the personal relationship side of life. I am concerned about people. With that strength, there are some different things that I could have done, from being a business owner, as I am, to being a registered nurse or a counselor, or coach or any other people related opportunities that would fit well with my personality. Discovering our personality strengths helps us to determine which opportunities suit us best.

Too often we try to describe ourselves, and who we are by the roles we take on, and I think that is an unfortunate mistake. I think that limits our opportunities. However, in growing a team, it is important that we know the personality strengths of each team member so that we can build a robust and versatile team.

The Values Preference Indicator helps us understand what we value. This is also a very useful tool to help build a team that goes the distance. If we can understand our values and look for those opportunities where we are most encouraged and motivated, and we can do the same for our management team, we are more likely to have a team that will go the distance with us. If an individual's values are not engaged on a daily basis, there is a strong possibility that person will become dissatisfied with their working environment and with the work they are doing, or the people they are working with, and start to look for another opportunity. To know the values of your people, and to be able to fulfill those needs, is very rewarding for all involved.

One of my values is flexibility. Thus I would never fit well in an opportunity where I could not move around and where I did not have flexibility. There are many values and often we do not take the time to understand ourselves in this area, resulting in people being in frustrating areas of opportunity in the workforce or business.

The most common remark from people that are in areas where their values aren't being met is that they can't wait for retirement, or if they would win the lottery they would quit their job the next day. What a sad existence it is for these people. How much better to understand what we value and to fit ourselves in opportunities that meet our values.

Self-Worth Indicator is a good indicator to understand our satisfaction with our self. If one is not completely satisfied with who we are, and content with where you are in life, that can be a tough road to travel. The emotional cost and resulting effect of low self-worth can be very costly, and hinder the growth of oneself and their company. This indicator will help you understand the areas of opportunity that might need to be addressed.

As Christians, we have a responsibility to those with low self-worth to help them gain an understanding that they are wonderfully made, as we are all created in the image of God. As a Christian in business that is part of a team, we have an opportunity to help people actualize their full potential. That means getting to understand the other members of the team, helping them embrace and accept their weaknesses and helping them to develop their strengths. Any team is as strong as its weakest link. Think on this: **"We who are strong ought to bear with the failings of the weak and not to please ourselves. Each of us should please our neighbors for their good, to build them up." (Romans 15:1-2).** We are here to build the Kingdom of God and if we believe that His Kingdom is within us, we ought to embody those beliefs.

Keep Dreaming

Dreams keep us stretched and are good to have so we can understand where we want to go. If we have a dream, then we can set objectives and goals for it. If we have a dream, we have something to strive for, to stretch towards, something to wake up for, something to live for.

I am a dreamer, and when a dream is realized, I consider the next dream. Ideally, we have a vision for every aspect of our life, something that keeps us stretched; something we strive for, something that is beyond our reach at the moment and will take careful planning and often some risk. Dreams keep the fire burning in our bellies.

For all the dreamers who may read this, take comfort in the fact that Joseph was a dreamer too and that it was his vision of Pharaoh's dream that built Pharaoh's empire and saved his family and millions of others from death and starvation. If Joseph didn't have a vision of what could be achieved, a whole nation of people would have come to ruin. The dreams of dreamers shape our world.

Also, when we are aware of our dreams, and the needed steps toward realizing our dreams, often something recognizable comes along that helps the dream come alive. I dare to dream. Do you?

The dream is something that forces us to look for creative ways and opportunities to meet an opportunity. The importance of having a dream is that when circumstances line up for us to move towards our dream, it is something we will recognize. I once had a dream to be an owner and operator of a truck. When the opportunity came to own a small trucking business, I recognized the opportunity. I was ready, and my dream was realized. I had another dream to one day be involved in business related to a Mission opportunity. I am now involved with one called Partners Worldwide where we coach and mentor small businesses in developing countries. I recognized the opportunity, and another dream was realized.

Dreams that stretch us towards a future for our businesses are also important. A dream is bigger than a goal. It is something that almost seems impossible today, but it is something we look forward to with an *'if it could be possible...'* approach. Write down your dreams. There is something about writing down, or writing out the dream that helps lock it into place and that helps us to recognize the pieces of it when they come to pass. You need to realize as well, that with God all things are possible. Simply put, no dream is impossible. The fact that you can even conceive such a dream in your imagination speaks to the fact that just maybe it is God that gave it to you in the first place.

When the Lord told Abram in Genesis 12:1-3 to, **"Go from your country, your people and your father's household to the land I will show you. "I will make you**

into a great nation, and I will bless you; I will make your name great, and you will be a blessing. I will bless those who bless you, and whoever curses you I will curse; and all peoples on earth will be blessed through you", if he did not believe in that dream of his future, all that we have come to know of the children of Israel, including Jesus Christ, would not have become a manifested reality. It is important to follow our dreams and to put God first in those dreams. It is also important to let God direct our lives. In essence, we are here to fulfill His mission and can only attain true happiness by living according to His will.

For I know the plans I have for you," declares the Lord, "plans to prosper you and not to harm you, plans to give you hope and a future. (Jeremiah 29:11). Share the vision you have in mind, always realizing, for it to materialize; it must be

God's plan for us.

Take a look at the story of Jonah who was bent on disobeying God's will, and God's dream and purpose for him.

Jonah was a prophet, who was giving the word of the Lord to the Israelites. The Lord spoke to him saying: **"Go to the great city of Nineveh and preach against it, because its wickedness has come up before me." (Jonah 1:2)**

Jonah did not want to preach to the people of Nineveh because they were the enemies of his land. He wanted Nineveh to die in its sins, and not turn to God and live. So Jonah went to Joppa and took a ship for Tarshish and not Nineveh.

But the Lord saw Jonah on the ship, and the Lord sent a great storm that seemed as if it would break the ship in pieces. The sailors threw overboard everything on the ship; and when they could do no more, every man prayed to his god to save the ship and themselves. But Jonah was fast asleep. The ship's captain came to him, and said: **"How can you sleep? Get up and call on your god! Maybe he will take notice of us so that we will not perish." (1:6)**

Jonah told them he was the cause of the storm. The ship's crew wanted to know more about him. So, they asked, **"Tell us, who is responsible for making all this trouble for us? What kind of work do you do? Where do you come from? What is your country? From what people are you?" (1:8)**

Then Jonah told them the whole story, how he came from the land of Israel, and that he had fled away from the presence of the Lord. And they said to him: **"What should we do to you to make the sea calm down for us?" (1:11)**

Then said Jonah: **"Pick me up and throw me into the sea, and it will become calm. I know that it is my fault that this great storm has come upon you." (1:12)**

But the men were not willing to throw Jonah into the sea. They rowed hard to bring the ship to the land, but they could not. Then they cried unto the Lord, and said: **"Please, Lord, do not let us die for taking this man's life. Do not hold us accountable for killing an innocent man, for you, Lord, have done as you pleased." (1:14)**

At last, when they could do nothing else to save themselves, they threw Jonah into the sea. Immediately the storm ceased, and the waves became still. Then the men on the ship feared the Lord greatly. They offered a sacrifice to the Lord and made promises to serve him.

We serve God best when we obey His will and share his vision. Let us not be like Jonah who was swallowed up by a whale when he was thrown overboard and spat out in Nineveh. What commission has God given you to fulfill?

Shared Vision of what you want to achieve and an understanding of what you want to accomplish with your company is important for you and for the people that work with you. If your people do not understand where you want to go, they will be challenged to go forward themselves with confidence and excitement. This can result in a feeling of insecurity. If everyone understands the mission and the vision and they buy into it, the result provides for a rich experience and will engage everyone in getting to where you want to go. If they understand and buy in, they will enthusiastically help you get there.

3
Acknowledging Others Ability To Contribute To The Building of Your Team

1 Corinthians 12:12-14
Just as a body, though one, has many parts, but all its many parts form one body, so it is with Christ. For we were all baptized by one Spirit so as to form one body—whether Jews or Gentiles, slave or free—and we were all given the one Spirit to drink. Even so the body is not made up of one part but of many.

As business people and children of the Kingdom of God, we should acknowledge the input of others. We should not begrudge anyone a compliment. For as the Apostle Paul says in 1 Corinthians 12:12-14, the church is one body made up of many units. We all should exemplify one God, as we are of one spirit and one accord. We are one team.

The early church understood teamwork. That was how they spread the gospel in a time that preaching and teaching Jesus cost them their lives. King Herod was arresting those who belonged to the church to persecute them. James, the brother of John, was put to death with the sword and he was looking to seize Peter also. This happened during the Festival of Unleavened Bread. When Herod arrested Peter, he put him in prison, which was guarded by many soldiers. Herod intended to try and kill Peter after the Passover. While Peter was in jail, the members of the church were earnestly praying to God to rescue him.

On the night before the trial, Peter was sleeping between two soldiers, bound with two chains, and sentries stood guard at the entrance when suddenly an angel of the Lord appeared, and a light shone in the cell. He woke Peter told him to get up, and the chains fell off Peter's wrists. The angel told him to get dressed and to wrap himself and follow him.

When Peter was following the angel out of prison, he had no idea that what the angel was doing was not a vision.; so surreal was the experience. They passed the first and then the second set of guards before coming to the iron gate leading to the city. It opened for them by itself, and they went through it. When they had walked the length of one street, suddenly the angel left him. That was when Peter came to himself. He said, **"Now I know without a**

doubt that the Lord has sent his angel and rescued me from Herod's clutches and from everything the Jewish people were hoping would happen." (Acts 12:11)

Because the church was united they were praying for him and he was able to go to the house of Mary, the mother of John, also called Mark, where many people had gathered and were praying for him, Peter. **Peter knocked at the outer entrance, and a servant named Rhoda came to answer the door. 14 When she recognized Peter's voice, she was so overjoyed she ran back without opening it and exclaimed, "Peter is at the door!" (Acts 12:13-14)**

This is how we must operate, as a team, as the early church did. In business, it is the same as it is with the church, especially if you a follower of Christ and living for the Kingdom of God.

Andrew Carnegie, who was a very wealthy industrialist in his time, believed in the collective strength of others to make up a strong team. One of my favorite quotes from Andrew Carnegie is (I will quote this several times):

"Never be so foolish as to not surround yourself with people smarter than yourself."

To accomplish this, we need a level of humility that allows the strengths, skills and abilities of others to shine. As a business owner, if you can eliminate a level of pride that might be preventing you from engaging the expertise of others, and engage the strengths of those around you, you will be better by it. This is an important step towards freedom. Without that transition, people sometimes struggle for years to put a team of good people together. James 4:6 tells us "But he gives us more grace. God opposes the proud but shows favor to the humble."

Romans 15:1 also tells us, **"We who are strong ought to bear with the failings of the weak and not to please ourselves."** This means we have a responsibility as Christian leaders to build the weakest links on our team. It is not enough to just be the leader. To grow our team, we must have an interest in developing its members.

If employees are not recognized, or encouraged for what they bring to the table, and are undervalued, there is an excellent chance that person is already looking for a new opportunity. You do not want to lose workers because they are not being challenged. This means a loss of the most valuable resource in the company – the people. Retaining employees is an important key to your success.

People often have much to offer and are usually very gifted in particular areas. If you respect others, those that have the skills that you are looking for to build your team, and you lift them up and bring them into an inner circle of opportunity to manage needed area of responsibilities, everyone wins. They will respect you, appreciate you, and work with you to meet your objectives, often as if they were running their own company. That is how you want to treat them; you want to treat them as shareholders, value them, lift them up, and allow them to shine.

Synergy is the power of collective thinking. This can be a great benefit when you start to engage the thinking of others. Teach people to think, encourage them when they come up with new ideas, and reward them for their thinking and ideas, and something beautiful starts to take shape.

Brainstorming for opportunities available around new ideas becomes a rewarding experience. We developed the **Business Building Team (BBT)** specifically for this opportunity. To engage strategic thinking around the future, and what it could look like, take those ideas and develop a strategic plan. It is very rewarding to see those ideas come to fruition.

When past experiences of others are sought out to provide creative solutions, the person called upon is honored, and your company benefits from that experience. Everybody wins.

Proverbs 11:14, "For lack of guidance a nation falls, but victory is won through many advisers."

This passage of scripture is a reminder to us that when we build each other up, we are creating a strong team. The aim of every team should be to reduce the weaknesses it may have that it may strive and continuously build upon its successes. When there are fewer weak links in our team, the wisdom of each member can be relied upon, and this makes the whole team stronger, not just for the company but the Kingdom of God. We are called to Shepherd to help steer His sheep by living by His example, and the small teams we build must embody mini-kingdoms of God.

Building a great Management Team is a major step towards your freedom as a business leader. And creating a culture that appreciates the contributions of your team is a crucial part of keeping the team together and growing.

Team Building

To ensure your business enjoys success, building a strong team is essential. One thing I do not like doing, and I am not good at, is reading the fine print in a contract. In the past, I often overlook reading the fine print and ended up signing at the bottom and trusting that all was well. One time I did that, and I discovered we were locked in a contract term that I was very unhappy with. It was a five-year contract with an automatic rollover for another five years unless we gave the right amount of notice before the contract ending. I noted the date that the contract notice needed to be given and watched very carefully for that date. And when the time arrived I dutifully gave my notice and the contract ended. I was finally satisfied and felt relieved.

A short time later, a representative from the same company came by to talk to me about continuing to service our account. I told him I was very unhappy with their contract terms for their service and for that reason had no desire to continue. He assured me that was no problem and that they would be willing to service our account without a contract.

The service resumed without a contract, and I was satisfied. Some months later, I was given a stack of documents to sign and once again, without realizing it. I signed the same contract document, entering into the same contract once again. I didn't know that I had signed this contract until a few years later when we wanted to engage a new contractor at a much lower offered price. It was then that I was reminded by this current contractor that I had signed an agreement with them. I was so frustrated, I canceled their service, refused to pay their invoices and yes in time ended up in court. In the end, we settled out of court. My point with this little story is that I need somebody on my team that enjoys and is willing to read the fine print on the contract. This, and many other responsibilities, can be taken on by others that enjoy doing what they are responsible for. And then the business can enjoy a safe, healthy environment that allows it to conduct business without as many challenges.

There are quite a number of responsibilities that we are not that good at, but when we engage others, they do what they enjoy best, and we all benefit from that. As faith leaders, we coach others to their fullest potential. We benefit by gaining more time for ourselves when we leave certain decision-making responsibilities in the right capable hands, and we also benefit by watching those we nurture grow.

Who Makes The Decisions?

There was a time I made most decisions on my own, whether they were a change in business opportunity, purchase of an asset, or acquisition of property, I would do the best I could to assess the benefit and value and make the best decision I could make. That of course often led to decisions that were not as good as they could have been. Some of those decisions cost us many thousands of dollars. Other decisions caused us headaches and frustrations.

One example is a small business that I started for all the wrong reasons. That little business, because it was started for the wrong reasons, was not researched properly and was not set up correctly; in short, there were many reasons all the way around that caused it to fail. It was wasted energy, wasted dollars, and in the end a failed business. That could have been avoided if we had a team approach to researching properly all that needed to be done, and by putting the right people in place from the outset. It was very likely we would have either not started the business or, after having done the due diligence and discovering there was a real opportunity, that business would have had a greater opportunity to enjoy success.

What I am trying to let you grasp is how valuable an asset other people are to any company. Many times we have issues trusting others, but trust is powerful when harnessed. It is crucial we remember that all knowledge is not encompassed in any one individual but is rather woven into a network of people. It is important that we keep in our minds that God created many different people and to each, He gave different talents. As a team leader, the goal is harvesting those talents to bear fruit for the team. As a child living in the Kingdom of God, we must understand that investing our talents means investing in others and watching them bear fruit for God. Otherwise, we are like the man in the parable who buried his talent.

Everybody has a unique gift, and everybody has something to contribute. As a leader, your greatest responsibility is to pull that gift out, harness it, and create opportunities for it to work and be developed:

For this reason I remind you to fan into flame the gift of God, which is in you through the laying on of my hands. (2 Timothy 1:6)

Paul understood the importance of bringing to the fore what was gifted to those he mentored. When God said, **"It is not good for man to be alone" (Genesis 2:18)** it was a multi-faceted statement that would be applicable even in business. The whole idea of humanity is built on unity, and we are made to function within a community, with each member uniquely gifted, with a very particular contribution to make to the whole.

A good leader knows how to identify what others can bring to the table, and give them an opportunity to make it good, even if they make mistakes along the way. Many are afraid to delegate responsibility because of fear of failure, but the road to success is paved with failure. That is how we became leaders in the first place. We don't want others to make the same mistakes we do, but it is often an unavoidable part of the process that we have to endure patiently.

4
Trusting And Respecting Others

1 Peter 2:17
Show proper respect to everyone, love the family of believers, fear God, honor the emperor.

You cannot build an efficient team without knowing their strengths. You can take a chance and hope that you have the right strengths, wait and see if your best guess is accurate, go with your gut, or you can use an effective method of using Personality Style Indicators (PSIs).

Your management team should consist of Division Operation Managers, Office Manager, Accountant or Controller, Marketing and Sales, and the Leader, Supervisor, and Manager of the other teams you may have within your company. Within the management team, you will have people that have creative abilities, organizing abilities, financial planning abilities, strong leadership abilities, communication strengths, and people skills.

You need to know what is important for your company and every business is somewhat different. In our company, for instance, we have some unique and various services. Thus we have Division Managers on our team. We also have heavy equipment, for which the continuous operation takes specialized knowledge and understanding, so we have an Equipment Manager. Our management team is made up of our Office Manager that manages office procedures and office staff. We have Division Operation Managers that are responsible for the operations of that division as well as strategic planning and day-to-day management to grow our opportunities, manage sales and marketing, and our accountant/controller.

Our Equipment Manager is responsible for keeping our equipment in good operating condition, to look at replacing and updating equipment and other responsibilities on a day-to-day basis. Our Controller is responsible for accounting duties, providing financial information to assist each Division Manager to manage their responsibilities. Our Sales Manager keeps us updated on upcoming challenges to prepare for, etc.

Thus, in understanding our needs we have been able to assemble a team of people with particular strengths that contribute towards their responsibilities as well as enjoy what they are called to do.

Organizations are made up of ordinary human beings together performing better than they could on their own. Trust and encouragement bring out whatever strength there is in its members, and they use each person's strength to help all the others perform at their best. The purpose of an organized team is to enable common people to do uncommon things.

One of the challenges of many small businesses today is it fails to recognize the values of its individual members and in so doing it fails to function as a team. Often there are situations where a few people, often very gifted, are trying to do all or most of the work. This is completely contrary to the teachings of the Scripture and always leads to inefficiency and failure in teaching people the communal values of the Bible, even when there is an organizational success. No matter how gifted or capable, the ones who think they need no one else or no matter how we believe that we are indispensable, that is not the case. No person is an island. A teamwork mentality is another one of the qualities of maturity.

Jesus is our perfect example and teacher. One might think that Jesus, of all people, would not have trusted the help of others to accomplish the things the Father had sent Him to do. He could calm the storms, raise the dead, heal the sick, make the blind see and the lame walk, bind the demonic, forgive sin, and even call ten thousand angels to His aid, yet He still enlisted a team of disciples.

We may wonder how Jesus could ever use them. They were impulsive, temperamental, easily offended, and had all the prejudices of their environment. They were fishermen and from varying different backgrounds unrelated to the missionary works they were about to carry out. These men were selected by the Lord to be His assistants. They represent an average cross-section of the people we have to work with today.

Jesus saw in these men the potential for transforming the world. This was what they did when they learned to work together as a team for the kingdom of God. Thus, at the very outset of His ministry, Christ called a small team of twelve men to be with Him for training and to whom He also delegated responsibilities (see Mark 1:14-18; 3:13-19). Jesus' team of disciples was hardly the epitome of success in the early part of their ministry, but after the Lord's ascension and the coming of the Spirit of God, history demonstrates how this first-century team of men became tremendously successful as they went forth to spread the message of the gospel. They not only led people to Christ but invested and multiplied themselves in others in a great team effort. Thus, by His very methods, the Lord Jesus illustrates the essential principle of teamwork and being a team player. If we are to grow, mature, and follow in His footsteps, we must learn to become team players whether leaders or followers. We must learn to see the values of others despite their flaws and weaknesses.

Matthew 7:12 says, **"So in everything, do to others what you would have them do to you, for this sums up the Law and the Prophets."** If we learn to treat each other with respect, we will start seeing their benefits to others and ourselves.

To respect everyone, believers must be conscious that God has created all people in His image, regardless of whether they believe in Christ or not. We should show them proper respect and honor because their souls are of more value than all the wealth in the world (Luke 10:33-34; 1 Corinthians 10:33).

Loving those in the Kingdom of God means to love all, regardless of color, nationality, opinions, or affiliations. We are to demonstrate to the world that we love all people, in Christ. The apostle John wrote of this principle a number of times. Quoting Jesus, he writes, **"A new command I give you: Love one another. As I have loved you, so you must love one another. 35 By this everyone will know that you are my disciples, if you love one another." (John 13:34-35).**

We recently had an email from an atheist asking if we only hired Christians. Our reply was that we hire based on skill and ability, not on religious affiliation. I like to be inclusive of all. And then we encourage the love of Christ through us to affect those who are yet unsurrendered.

5

Clearing The Chaos: Organizing To Clarity

**1 Corinthians 14:40
But everything should be done in a
fitting and orderly way.**

It was 2006; we were successful in winning a major contract in preparation for the 2010 Olympics. I soon realized that this work would cause us to have busier periods than we had ever experienced, and more people on staff than ever before. We would also have more important responsibilities, and the need to be more organized was very evident.

Up until this point, we did not have anything visibly displaying our Workflow, often referred to as a Workflow Chart, Organizational Chart, or simply an Org Chart. After one of our Safety Meetings, I was discussing some of our new opportunities and challenges with our Safety Coordinator, Roy Allen. Roy shared that he was familiar with the work involved in working through the process of putting together an Org Chart and the accompanying

Job Descriptions needed for each role. I had come to know Roy as a man I could trust. We quickly came to an agreement on how we would work together on this new project.

Roy and I started to discuss the various roles that were important to our business and how the organizational chart should flow. It took some time for us to work it through, but eventually we had the beginnings of how we thought to best organize ourselves for efficient work processes and effective communication throughout our business.

I soon realized however that although the positions highlighted were needed, our business was somewhat unique. We had at least four different business services all interwoven under one company banner. That made the organizational chart that we had initially put together a bit awkward.

Some weeks later I was having a conversation with Clarence, a friend of mine, who owns a successful Chrysler dealership in Lethbridge, Alberta. I asked him how he organized his business. It was in this conversation that clarity came to me, and I understood how our organizational chart needed to be revised and reassembled.

We almost entirely tore apart the original one we had worked on and began to reassess how best to put this hybrid together. The resulting organizational chart, except for a few minor revisions, once it was rebuilt, served us very well for the next ten years.

An Organizational chart needs to be reassessed periodically to ensure it still serves the company's needs. Each company's needs are somewhat different; thus an Org Chart will be a little different for every business, but it is a crucial documented process that you need to have for your successful business.

You need to understand the various roles and responsibilities that are required, to whom they are responsible, how they work together, and how the teams communicate. Without a good communication flow, and a clear understanding of the role and accompanying responsibility, efficient workflow is challenged, with an excellent possibility that chaos will be part of your regular work day.

It is important that when anybody that comes to your business, whether they be a vendor, client or employee, and is looking for clarification on a particular aspect of your business, that there is no confusion as to who is responsible for that particular responsibility.

There's nothing worse than people pointing fingers at each other when something did not happen the way it should, and the blame game starts. You, as a business owner, need to eliminate this confusion, and the best way to start eliminating that confusion is with an organizational chart. This takes some time to develop, and it starts with really understanding the needs of your business.

The organizational chart makes it clear who is responsible for what, who reports to who, who assists each manager or supervisor in their roles, who supports one another in their roles within their teams. The organizational chart should eliminate confusion, and bring clarity to every aspect of your business. It will allow for smooth operations on a day-to-day basis.

Take the time to reacquaint yourself with your organizational chart often, and make changes and adjustments as you go. It should be a living document, not something you put away and never look at again. Your employees should know who they report to, and each member of every team should be clear as to how they function within the business. It is also recommended that you carefully talk this through so that people reporting to a particular supervisor understand from whom they receive direction. Working out the reporting structure carefully, with clarity, will avoid much confusion.

In organizing your organizational chart, you need to carefully think through what teams are important. Wherever there are varied roles with accompanying responsibilities, consider building a team around that. That team will need someone to lead them or someone that is responsible for direction and leadership. You must work your way to an organized approach to day-to-day responsibilities.

The objective of your organizational chart is to eliminate the confusion when there is an inquiry around who is in charge of a particular area. There should be no confusion when anyone is looking for the person responsible for a particular opportunity. If there is confusion, it is time to go back to the organizational chart and review it. As with a cabinet shuffle, there will be a need at times to reassign and clarify responsibilities for the various people assigned leadership responsibility.

Think through and identify the various roles and accompanying responsibilities that will allow for your business to serve your clients with excellence. Clearly articulate the responsibilities ascribed to each role through a job description. The more clarity around responsibilities and expectations, the more freedom you will enjoy, and the more valued the team member feels. Review this area carefully, and frequently, especially in the beginning.

Organizational charts' design and structure can differ greatly depending on the needs of your business. Take the time to look at organizational charts of other companies, and talk to people who have organized themselves. Get a good understanding of the various needs of your company. Do not hasten this process as it is one of the most significant opportunities of getting you as a business owner to both enjoy your business, and allow others in your business to enjoy their responsibilities, while working towards an ever more effective shared management organization.

The time we spend on our organizational chart and organizing it properly was probably some of the best and eventually most rewarding time that we spent in moving us forward as a team. We built and rebuilt our organizational chart a number of occasions in getting it right. It was never an easy process, but in the end, it has been a very rewarding exercise. Don't rush this opportunity. Take time to think.

Once you have got your chart together in what you think it should be, look at it over and over again. Walk through the structures of responsibility, who reports to who, who communicates with whom, and how the team is best served. Ask every possible question until you have clarity. Do this with your management team and make sure that everyone, as much as possible, agrees that the flow is right, that it feels good, and that it serves its purpose.

Once you identify the various roles, you need to clearly define job or role descriptions and expectations and write them down. This allows for discussion leading to agreement and avoids assumptions that could lead to frustration, and possibly anger. Be responsible for yourself and others, and take the time to get this right.

The organizational chart should not tell you 'who's boss.' Personally, I don't like the term 'boss' although it is likely one of the terms that are most clearly understood. I like to work as a team. I have my responsibilities; one of my responsibilities is to identify areas of need for the team members that I serve. I serve them, and in serving them, it is my duty to ask them; *"How can I help you?"* People that create organizational charts to help identify who serves them, as in "I am the boss, and you serve me" will be losing more opportunity than they gain. Those that rightly understand the role of leadership and the purpose of the organizational chart will gain the most freedom and enjoyment in their business. While there is no denying that the mantle of leadership does fall inevitably on the leader, how that mantle is worn will have a noticeable impact, positive or negative, on those around you.

The Bible speaks of the church's organizational structure within the New Testament. These include its ultimate leader, its human leaders, its members, and its relationship with other churches.

The head of the church is Jesus Christ. Ephesians 1:22 informs us that, **"And God placed all things under his feet and appointed him to be head over everything for**

the church." He is the great shepherd (Hebrews 13:20) and leader of the flock of God.

At the second tier of leadership, the New Testament notes the existence of two groups of leaders—the elders and the deacons. First Peter 5:1-4 also teaches that elders are to serve as shepherds of God's people and to live as examples among them.

The New Testament recognizes the importance of church members and that each member is expected to regularly gather together (Hebrews 10:25), to grow (Acts 2:42), serve others, and share their faith.

Churches are to live in harmony with other churches and to live as salt and light to the unbelieving world. The early churches shared the same core beliefs and often helped one another through finances or encouragement, serving as an example for today's churches.

When Moses became the leader of the children of Israel and all others who he led out of Egypt, he too had to create an organizational structure.

In Exodus 18:13-27 an account is given that on a particular day, **Moses took his seat to serve as judge for the people, and they stood around him from morning till evening. When his father-in-law saw all that Moses was doing for the people, he said, "What is this you are doing for the people? Why do you alone sit as judge, while** all these people stand around you from morning till evening?" Moses answered him, "Because the people come to me to seek God's will. Whenever they have a dispute, it is brought to me, and I decide between the parties and inform them of God's decrees and instructions." Moses' father-in-law replied, "What you are doing is not good. You and these people who come to you will only wear yourselves out. The work is too heavy for you; you cannot handle it alone. Listen now to me and I will give you some advice, and may God be with you. You must be the people's representative before God and bring their disputes to him. Teach them his decrees and instructions, and show them the way they are to live and how they are to behave. But select capable men from all the people—men who fear God, trustworthy men who hate dishonest gain—and appoint them as officials over thousands, hundreds, fifties and tens. Have them serve as judges for the people at all times, but have them bring every difficult case to you; the simple cases they can decide themselves. That will make your load lighter, because they will share it with you. If you do this and God so commands, you will be able to stand the strain, and all these people will go home satisfied." Moses listened to his father-in-law and did everything he said. He chose capable men from all Israel and made them leaders of the people, officials over thousands, hundreds, fifties and tens. They served as judges for the people at all

times. The difficult cases they brought to Moses, but the simple ones they decided themselves. Then Moses sent his father-in-law on his way, and Jethro returned to his own country.

Not only did Moses create an organization structure, but he also listened to the counsel of his father-in-law who was much wiser on the matter. Likewise, we are called to humble ourselves and listen to those who know more than we do in a particular area so that the work of the Kingdom of God may continue reaping souls for the Kingdom.

6
Hiring Strategically

Hebrews 11:6
And without faith it is impossible to please God, because anyone who comes to him must believe that he exists and that he rewards those who earnestly seek him.

If you want to build a strong team, start hiring strategically. Develop a process that identifies and qualifies the team's need, and the right candidates to fill that need. One employee will be very different from another employee. You also need to identify the roles and responsibilities of the particular opportunity at hand, the types of clients they will serve, the jobs they will do, and dictate the style and personality needed to meet the needs of all involved effectively.

To assist our team leaders to hire effectively, we use a Job Style Indicator (JSI). This takes the guess work out of deciding the most effective method for a particular responsibility. This is an excellent tool to use when you first start building your management team. Character, style, and skill are all different, and they are all important.

A properly laid out hiring process should be written out, clearly understood and agreed to by everyone involved. We are responsible to those who take the time to apply to our companies for a position to treat them and their time with respect. The unsuccessful applicant that has come all the way through our hiring process should leave more confident than when they first came. We cannot hire every applicant that we interview, but we can encourage them as they continue their search.

I encourage the applicant to interview us as well, just to be sure that we can provide for their needs, and satisfy their core values as a company. They will need to know what we offer a successful candidate, as we need to know their potential contribution. Take away as many unanswered questions as possible, allowing for candidates to make right decisions as it relates to where they contribute their skills and abilities.

Once a person has been hired, a very important part of the process is to do reviews in the first months of the new hires tenure. The new team member should have the opportunity to correct areas of concern where they are possibly misunderstanding their responsibilities. From the beginning, the new employee needs to agree to ongoing coaching and encouragement towards getting the job done right.

As detailed as the hiring process may be, there will always be room for improvement, and there will always be people that don't work out. There should be no surprise with the new employee that isn't working out. If the final decision is that the new employee is not suited for the position, or if the review process is engaged in responsibly, the employee will only agree with you that they are better suited in a different role.

I suggest a six-month probation so that adequate time is given for the new team member to make the corrections that are needed to prove that they can take on the responsibility required. Having the right attitude is a priority for us. I have found that with the right attitude there are very few people who don't become outstanding team members. I have also found that with a poor attitude there are very few people that become excellent team members.

Once an employee has been with the company for one year, a 360 review is generated. This review allows for a more formal approach to review an employee's performance. This is an opportunity to be reviewed by their peers. This review should be repeated annually for all employees. Ideally, this should be a time of encouragement. Each employee reviewed will have agreed on areas to correct, improve and grow in. Also, each employee reviewed should leave a review with confirmation that in certain areas they are excelling and their contribution is appreciated and is encouraging to others.

We do not fire people. We like to release the people that don't work out to their new future. Not every person is suited for every position. There will be times, despite our best efforts, that someone will be ill-suited for the job they were hired for. It should not be a surprise to the employee that they are not well-suited to the position. There should have been ongoing dialogue around the improvements needed. If the improvements cannot be attained and the employee, at some point, is deemed unsuitable for the position, they should be released with dignity. Each person has value. Ideally, the person released, with our encouragement, will more quickly discover the opportunity they should seek out for themselves elsewhere. If we have taken the time we should have, they should be clearer on where they would be best suited to make that contribution.

It should be noted as well, that to be truly responsible for helping people to live purposefully, we are reminded that we may be doing a disservice to a certain employee, as they may not on their own have the risk capacity to venture out and discover their best employment opportunity. Often it is when people are pushed beyond their comfort zones that they discover the best that is available to them, and in the process bless and benefit everyone else close to them, as they finally start living.

I always strive towards clarity of strength in contribution for each person reporting to me. If we know our strengths and build on them, we will make valuable contributions. If we can be a strength-finder for another, even though they might not stay with us, we often have made an encouraging difference.

7

Organizing Further to Reduce and Hopefully Eliminate Unneeded Challenges

Psalm 127:1-2
Unless the Lord builds the house, the builders labor in vain. Unless the Lord watches over the city, the guards stand watch in vain. In vain you rise early and stay up late, toiling for food to eat — for he grants sleep to those he loves.

Let us say it is Monday morning, and you know it is going to be a busy day. There are important meetings throughout the day, and a lot has to get done. You are excited because new opportunities are about to surface. You come into the office and check the messages that have come in over the weekend. There are a variety of different messages, and then you come to the one that changes everything for the day. One of your staff members has called in sick, and there is no one to take his/her place. The choice you have is to take up her responsibilities and cancel all the meetings you had planned, or allow chaos to reign throughout that day while you have your important meetings. There is no easy choice.

To avoid this challenge being a repeat offender, one very good recommendation is to have a backup employee for every key position. It will still be a challenge when a key staff member is missing. People will have to work harder, but the important tasks will get done. Some less important tasks may have to wait for a day or so, but that which cannot wait will get done. Cross train a backup person for any position of importance which is vital to the company's well-being. This allows for emergencies to be looked after, vacations to be enjoyed without huge amounts of stress associated with the waiting pile of work when one gets back. Your clients will also continue to be looked after. This also avoids the potential threat by any one employee to maliciously upset your organization if they didn't get their way in something, which can sometimes occur.

Cross training for a variety of positions and responsibilities should be encouraged. At times there is fear that if someone is cross trained for 'my' position, 'my' employment may be in jeopardy. That is a fear that should be removed from anyone's thinking and what should replace it is that an employee with the ability and willingness to cross train another employee is a much more valuable employee. A cross-trained employee should receive recognition and increased remuneration for their efforts. This should encourage others to seek the opportunity to be cross-trained. The more cross-trained employees you have, the better off your entire company will be for it. That said, the employees that train others should be continuously encouraged for the value they bring to their team.

Committees With Purpose

Outside of the daily responsibilities at work, there is a need for a variety of focuses that can be well served by committees. Some that come to mind would be a safety committee, a social committee, or any purpose and focus in addition to regular work responsibilities that could make a considerable difference for your company.

If you have employees that would like to make a bigger difference, a contribution of value, and there may not be a position to engage them full time, participating on a committee will be a good step forward. These employees as well can be observed more carefully for leadership capabilities, and when the opportunity presents, can assist in covering for another leader on an 'as needed' basis.

We recently introduced a new committee called our Employee Management Committee. A member of each team throughout our business combined with a few of our management team, each on a rotating basis to encourage eventual participation by all. We are anticipating that this will increase effective communication and bring good ideas from staff to be considered and discussed and if deemed to be helpful, to be implemented.

The Employee Handbook

How do we answer the questions that may be wondered about by an employee or an applicant for a vacant position? Important questions they may feel they have no right to ask, or time is limiting them to ask some but not all questions. How are as many questions answered as possible? How do we address the issue of culture within a business?

When Peter VanGiesen came on staff, he started asking questions to help him and myself gain clarity on policies, procedures, and more. It soon became apparent that some of us understood what was important, but it was buried within our minds but was uncovered one question at a time. This is not a good way to gain clarity.

As well, without this information being written down, I had to admit there were many times we ran into situations where there were multiples of variations on a given policy, leading to confusion and frustrations.

It was Peter's suggestion that we put together an Employee Hand Book, a booklet where as much as is important at

Denbow could be recorded and when needed, discovered by anyone interested with relative ease.

This became one of Peter's projects, and even with the help of an assistant and a software program designed to discover what needed to be included, was still a lengthy, but very rewarding initiative.

All the questions that any employee might ask concerning policy towards employee concerns should be found in the employee handbook. There is software available that helps to put this handbook together and asks the various questions that need clarification for any employee of the company. This tool is a tremendous contribution towards stability and satisfaction of employees around any issue about their employment. I like to give a copy to applicants that make it through to the final decision of accepting a position with us before they make the final decision. If they take the time to review our policy around their concern carefully, and they agree to it, we will have a much more satisfied employee long term, taking away more of the risk of eventual dissatisfaction due to wrong understanding. Doing as much as possible to lower attrition leads to a stronger happier company of people, and toward your freedom to enjoy your business.

Another important consideration to evaluate regarding the value of a well written Employee Handbook is the comfort of the employee's significant others. If a business and the way it treats its employees can be assessed, and a level of comfort gained by family members or significant others, the prospective employee could make better decisions as well, with the encouragement of those around them.

It is our duty as Christians to consider the family just as the church is a family. By treating the employee as if he has autonomy, he or she can make plans and build their families. As Christians, we should remember who heads our homes.

Joshua 24:15, But if serving the Lord seems undesirable to you, then choose for yourselves this day whom you will serve, whether the gods your ancestors served beyond the Euphrates, or the gods of the Amorites, in whose land you are living. But as for me and my household, we will serve the LORD.

As members of the greater Christian family, we are here to serve the Lord. As servants of the Lord, we have a responsibility to nurture healthy minds within the home.

As much as we are business people, we cannot put money before everything. We must recognize that as Christians everything comes secondary to the home. If the spouse and children are not happy, the employee is not likely to be happy either. With God at the helm, we can nurture a happy home.

Genesis 33:5, Then Esau looked up and saw the women and children. "Who are these with you?" he asked. Jacob answered, "They are the children God has graciously given your servant."

Children are the most precious gifts in a home. They are blessings from God. Where there is discontent in a home, it reflects on the attitude of the employee. Every company benefits when the homes of the employees are happy places and when employees feel they can make plans for their children, they are better able to function within the workplace.

As Christians and kingdom dwellers we have an opportunity to cherish the family of God by treating our homes and offices as His mini-Kingdom. We must remember the sacrifice that was made to let us come to know the heavenly Father.

Galatians 4:4-7 says, **"But when the set time had fully come, God sent his Son, born of a woman, born under the law, to redeem those under the law, that we might receive adoption to sonship. Because you are his sons, God sent the Spirit of his Son into our hearts, the Spirit who calls out, "*Abba,* Father." So you are no longer a slave, but God's child; and since you are his child, God has made you also an heir."**

We must remember that God sacrificed His Son for us. That is how important the family is to Him. We were lost, and He sent His Son to redeem His lost children. We have a duty and a responsibility to protect and nurture the home, and as business leaders, we can do that by letting our employees know where they stand in the company so that they can plan for their futures and the futures of their families.

Psalms 127:3-5, Children are a heritage from the Lord, offspring a reward from him. Like arrows in the hands of a warrior are children born in one's youth. Blessed is the man whose quiver is full of them. They will not be put to shame when they contend with their opponents in court.

We have a responsibility as Christians to nurture these gifts from God, our children, and our homes are their foundations. The church has a responsibility to encourage them to come unto God; that is because families are the core social units in all communities around the world, and healthy individuals within healthy families are at the core of a healthy society.

So, children of our employees should be considered. I have seen businesses totally consume the life of an individual leaving no room for families. We have a unique opportunity as kingdom citizens to address and correct this, and it should be clearly outlined in the employee handbook.

8
Understanding Effective Delegation

John 13:34-35
"A new command I give you: Love one another. As I have loved you, so you must love one another. By this everyone will know that you are my disciples, if you love one another."

'The buck stops with me; I might as well do it myself. Isn't there anybody around here that does anything? Why am I always the last to leave?' These and similar statements and questions are an indicator that you seriously need to learn the art of delegating. You cannot do it all by yourself. If you continue to try, at some point you will hurt yourself and the organization because you are withholding opportunity from someone that would do very well at some of the tasks you have refused to let go. Some of the tasks you have hung onto are so menial that others are watching you and thinking you are way too overpaid for that particular task. That is not to say that periodically you would pitch in and help out at some

of the most mundane and menial tasks, however, what should be corrected is that you are the one doing all the mundane and menial tasks. Your time is too valuable for that.

Consider the life and ministry of Jesus. I believe the legacy He established is very applicable to business. On the one hand, the works He did could have only been done by Him. Who else was healing the sick, raising the dead, giving sight to the blind, etc? Jesus came, and He was doing all these marvelous things that He alone could do, seemingly. What He did eventually was remarkable. He delegated responsibility to 12, then to 70, then to 120 who carried the same anointing He did and performed the same works.

We also see this spiritual delegation being done during Moses time.

The LORD said to Moses: "Bring me seventy of Israel's elders who are known to you as leaders and officials among the people. Have them come to the tent of meeting, that they may stand there with you. I will come down and speak with you there, and I will take some of the power of the Spirit that is on you and put it on them. They will share the burden of the people with you so that you will not have to carry it alone. (Numbers 11:16-17)

Delegating responsibility is mandatory to effectiveness and success in any business. Have you ever stopped and calculated what you charge your company for your time? If you take all your bonuses, dividends, salary, small perks or large ones and add them all up, your hourly rate is likely one of the highest in the company. Would you hire someone at that rate to pick up the mail?

Where you spend your time should result in your company moving forward, with new objectives and new goals. Your business should be moving forward, and you should be one of the primary movers of the vision, ideas, new objectives, innovations, brainstorming, building a stronger team, coaching and equipping. All these things should be an important part of your responsibility.

One way to determine what you should keep, and what you should share or delegate to others is to keep track of what you do on a daily basis for a period of time. Make a detailed list of everything you do. Keep track of this for approximately four weeks. A four-week cycle would complete most of the business' essential functions on a regular basis.

At the end of the four weeks identify whether the tasks you have taken responsibility for are A, B, or C tasks. A-tasks would be those that you should be part of whether they are taken on by yourself or in conjunction with your team. B-tasks are those tasks that somebody else could take on if they were trained for it. C-tasks are those which anybody could do without any, or very little training.

The C-tasks should be the first to be delegated immediately. This will free up some time for you, depending on how many C-tasks you have taken on. The B-tasks should be carefully assessed and may very possibly allow for your team to become stronger as they are trained to take them on. In this transition, your management team will feel much more appreciated, and you will start to notice an increasingly efficient team. The A-tasks are tasks you have to keep yourself. These functions should be carefully assessed that they are truly A-tasks. There are some that should remain yours and yours alone. These are tasks that if you want to build a stronger team, you should consider sharing with some of your management team. This will take your management team to a new level and will allow you the freedom that you are looking for.

There may be a tendency among some of us that are struggling to delegate to be fearful of releasing some of the tasks that we have kept for ourselves. One of the fears that often surface is in making decisions alone. If that were to change, we would lose the privilege of making quick decisions. There may also be a fear of *"Who will I be if I am not the decision maker?"*

I had discovered some benefits when I took my decision-making process to a new level. In asking for the insights of others before I made a decision, and seeking as often as possible consensus, the process of making good decisions enabled our management team to make many decisions without me. I also discovered that they made better decisions collectively, which gave me a new found freedom. This allowed me more time to engage in other things. If I had retained the decision-making privilege to myself, I would have withheld from them the privilege of growing and learning the art of good decision-making, and I would have withheld from myself the freedom that was available to me.

As you develop your management team to become good at processing new ideas and making good decisions, you will discover that over time you will be less needed in the day-to-day function of your business.

Gradually, as your team takes on more and more responsibility, they will become better leaders and managers and the daily responsibilities will be taken care of in ways that exceed your previous experience. Your business will have the capacity to grow quicker and stronger, and if you have the right people on your team, the entire company will grow in ways you never imagined. What happens then is that you will have the opportunity to work 'on' your business rather than 'in' your business. Working 'on' your business takes you to a new level and allows you to dream and consider opportunities which you never had time to consider before. You will be able to review practices, processes, and policies, etc. by taking a more relaxed and focused approach towards those areas of business that are important. You will have the time to review the important parts of your business and consider whether they are in need of an upgrade or change. You will have a chance to consider whether the products and services you provide are meaningful and are providing you the return that you are looking for. You will take the time to review employee practices and hiring processes, review processes and any number of employee related policies that will allow for your team to grow stronger. You will take the time to review your quality controls, delivery processes, etc. and, finally, have the time to work on the important things while others enjoy the opportunity to work in your business, taking on responsibilities that you would have done yourself.

Gaining more personal time from our businesses also allows us to spend more personal time with God. Relationships take time. A relationship with God, while unlike other relationships, still follows the rules of other relationships in that we must spend the time to build a strong bond. The Bible is filled with comparisons to help us conceptualize our relationship with God, and we have good role models to follow. For example, Christ is depicted as the bridegroom, and the Church is depicted as the bride, and when it comes to marriage, marriage is two joining their lives as one. Such intimacy involves time spent alone with one another, just as intimacy with God requires time. Spending time alone with a loved one gives us the opportunity to truly come to know that person. Spending time alone with God is no different. When we are alone with God, we draw closer to Him and get to know Him in a different way than we do in group settings.

God desires **"alone time"** with us. He wants a personal relationship with us. He created us as individuals, and He knows us before we were created in the womb. God knows the intimate details of our lives, such as the number of hairs on our heads. He knows the sparrows individually, and **"you are worth more than many sparrows" (Matthew 10:29, 31).** He invites us to come to Him and know Him. When we desire to know God intimately, we will seek Him early and spend time with Him. It is always a good idea to spend time in devotion before starting your day. We will be like Mary, sitting at Jesus' feet listening to His voice, with a willingness to please Him by keeping His commandments. We will hunger and thirst for righteousness, and we will be filled.

Perhaps the best reason for us to spend time alone with God is to follow biblical examples. In the Old Testament, we see God calling prophets to come to Him alone. Moses met with God alone at the burning bush and then on Mt. Sinai. David, whose many Psalms reflect a confident familiarity with God, communed with Him while on the run from Saul. God's presence passed by as Elijah was in the cave. In the New Testament, Jesus spent time alone with God. Very often He would leave the 'business' of His mission to do so. Jesus instructed us to pray to God alone at times: **"…when you pray, go into your room, close the door and pray to your Father, who is unseen." (Matthew 6:6a).**[2]

All these great characters of the Bible developed a personal relationship with God by spending alone time with him. We are called to do the same.

The Bible promises us in **James 4:8a, "Come near to God and he will come near to you."** He is waiting for you. In fact, God is looking for opportunities to speak to you, if only you would slow down enough to listen attentively. What you hear will show you how to keep your life aligned with His purposes.

Tips For Your Alone Time With God

Psalm 100:4 tells us, **"Enter his gates with thanksgiving and his courts with praise; give thanks to him and praise his name."**

---

[2] http://www.gotquestions.org/alone-with-God.html

We can thank Him for His patience and forgiveness, thank Him for the privilege of coming into His presence and thank Him for what He has done in and with our lives in the last year. This can be done, even when you sit at your desk, and there is no one else around.

You say, *"I want to trust God, but I don't hear him."* To hear God, you have to get near God. You don't hear God when your mind is filled with a thousand other distractions.

The Bible says, **"Be still, and know that I am God." (Psalm 46:10).**

We hear God when we quiet the noise in our head and build a relationship with Him. We have the time; we just need to make it. Life in business can rob you of this privilege. I often hear people say, *"I don't have the time."* Time is not something you have, but something you make.

We all have the same amount of hours in each day. We read about many who have made an impact both in the world and for the Kingdom. The fact is, we have to be good stewards of the time we are given, and this applies especially to those who are entrepreneurs. When you take on the responsibility of managing your own time, you become accountable. You decide how the hours are spent, and you cannot ignore the vital expectation of Our Father to spend time with Him, and with our families.

This is why delegating is so vital. It is not to say that you are incapable of doing it all.

The church can be viewed from the perspective of business. It can be regarded as an institution. So when Paul reiterates that it is made up of many members, with different functions, I believe He was speaking about business as well.

No business can succeed on the efforts of only one man, no more than the gospel can be spread through the nations by one man. When you start to delegate, you function as a bigger body, with a much wider reach. Time then becomes your servant, and you can easily manipulate it to include spending time doing what is even more important than making money.

9
Stop Assuming. Start Inspecting What You Expect

1 Corinthians 3:9
"For we are co-workers in God's service; you are God's field, God's building."

'Don't fix what ain't broke.'

'Let sleeping dogs lie.'

We have heard those statements many times. Unfortunately, what also lies within that statement is a hesitation to hold people accountable. What can result without some process of accountability is that if something isn't working at its best and it is not addressed and corrected, the best is never experienced. So how do we honor and respect those we have trained up and expect to do their jobs right without offending them by micromanaging them?

The business operating team is a group of people tasked with managing and leading others to ensure that the daily responsibilities of the business are carried out. I encourage regular Business Operating Team (BOT) meetings, which allows for update reports on new objectives, an opportunity to share a challenge and ask for feedback and advice, share new target goals, and to have the team hold each other accountable to the same. Team meetings are a must and need to happen regularly. How regular will differ with each team, and will in some ways depend on how responsive and responsible the team is to their assigned tasks, as agreed to by themselves and team. If team members walk away from a meeting, get agreed on tasks completed with little accountability, fewer meetings are necessary. If you discover however that team members may be too busy to take on some other self-assigned tasks, and some tasks may drift off course, more frequent meetings may be necessary.

The Business Building Team (BBT) has a different responsibility. The team may be comprised of some of the same members of the BOT team, but the focus is different. The focus of the BBT is to look forward and to come up with and discuss ideas that look at the future of the company's products or services. On this team, you need creative thinkers and visionaries. This team will assess, by discussion and research, the validity of the new ideas.

At times there will be a brainstorming session where every idea is a good idea until proven otherwise. Ideas should always be encouraged, for without thought towards new ideas, new services, new products, new procedures, and new processes a company cannot grow and it will not survive against a strong competitor in the long term. This team has the responsibility to review every aspect of future business practices, marketing, sales practices, products and service changes and updates or new products and services, employee-related programs, etc. This is a team for the creative thinker. It's an opportunity to reward those who love to think, and who love to come up with new ideas and see them grow. This team managed, respected and appreciated properly will bring much new life and opportunities to your business.

For all teams, accountability to the other team members is very important. An agenda for each meeting is important, and minutes recording various decisions made by team members need to be assembled and circulated. Your job as acting General Manager becomes much easier with accountability to the team in place. You won't have to micromanage each individual towards their success. The team will do that with you. If someone has agreed to complete a task by a certain date and it's not done, it will be much more effective to have the team hold that person accountable for completion. You will want your team to learn how to conduct themselves in an ongoing manner without you micromanaging individuals. Rather, you become their encourager, their coach, finding ways that you can assist them where they are asking for insight, and not hinder them from managing their responsibilities.

Likewise, as builders of God's church, we must hold ourselves accountable. We are His team. Teamwork is all around us in life. We see it in marriages, businesses, neighborhoods, and in our churches. God loves to see Christians working together submitting to His will. Consider your business as a local grocery mart. There is one store, but there are many different departments within that store. One department can do things another cannot, but they still have the same goal.

In the same way that the Kingdom is one body, with many members, so is your business; one body, many members, many different functions. God has blessed us all differently. Some people are preachers, givers, singers, advice givers, and some are prayer warriors. Some people are bolder, wiser, more confident, and have a stronger faith than others. We all have different abilities, but our primary goal is God and the advancement of His Kingdom. We fill in for our brothers & sisters where they need assistance.

In the church, there is not just one person micromanaging things. There is a collective team that works as one unit. That way the many gifts God has given us are allowed to shine.

We represent God wherever we are, and regardless of what we are doing, we should see ourselves as vessels, buildings, as temples of God. We carry Him into every sphere of life, and business.

10
Do Not Guess. Start Accounting For It

Matthew 11:28-30
"Come to me, all you who are weary and burdened, and I will give you rest. Take my yoke upon you and learn from me, for I am gentle and humble in heart, and you will find rest for your souls. For my yoke is easy and my burden is light."

'You cannot manage what you do not measure.'

This is a little saying that has a high degree of importance. You cannot make good decisions without the right financial information. You will be limited in your ability to borrow, and to grow an opportunity that is paying off. You won't know which area of your business is doing well, or which area of your business is costing you money. You will be guessing.

You may compare with others and decide to price merely by comparison with no useful information. You may decide on your employees pay by comparing with others, yet have no idea where you are at, where you are going and how you are going to get there. Without the proper measuring tools, and the accurate reports to help you make sense of where you are and where you are going, you will be stumbling in the dark hoping all is okay, like playing Russian roulette. Too many businesses have come to a sad end in their business life, and never understood what was going wrong. They thought all was well; they were busy, serving people, making widgets or whatever their business was, yet every month things were getting worse until they were no more than a faint memory. You cannot continue to grow a business without proper financial reporting in place.

I have discovered over the years that one of the areas many small business owners procrastinate in is the area of financial information and management systems. I have seen small business owners struggling to survive and come to realize they haven't sent out invoices sometimes for months. Getting behind on sending out invoices is a recipe for disaster. At times they may even become somewhat embarrassed, and due to the lapse of time, not send out an invoice, or they may have forgotten the details and under-estimate the cost of doing that particular piece of business, and then undercharge for the product or service.

Because they are busy each and every day, the fundamental aspects of financial responsibility of invoicing and receiving payment on time become just one extra burden. Then receivables slip further and further out, and clients, due to being busy, do not get that reminder that their account is overdue. Then accounts payable starts to suffer; vendors are calling for their money and unfortunately chaos reigns. Those are the days when a small business owner just wants to hide. The blame gets cast in many different directions; however, if that owner were to sit down and face the facts quietly, they would have to admit that there is a level of disorganization around finance.

I strongly encourage each and every business owner no matter what size they are to get their financial house in order. What seems like an unnecessary cost; to have someone skilled in the area of finance look after your business financial and administrative needs, will likely pale in comparison to the benefits you will receive. Keep in mind though that the details of your invoicing may require some of your input. However, getting your invoices sent out on time and following up with clients who have overdue receivables so that you can manage and pay your vendors on time, will be a huge relief and allow you to concentrate on that which you do best, grow your business.

Most entrepreneurs that I have met are not good accountants or bookkeepers. They do it because they think they are being responsible by keeping business expenses down. As a result, every aspect of their business suffers and may even be the reason their business fails. Had they focused on what they were best at, and leave that which they were not good at, they would still be in a healthy business. I strongly encourage you, if you are currently looking after your finances, to reassess this area of vital importance.

There are a few consistencies for virtually every business. You should know your monthly revenues, quarterly revenues, and yearly revenues as compared to the previous month, quarter and year. Measuring growth without that comparison will be difficult. Some will hone down into details such as daily and weekly metrics and comparatives. The least you should be measuring is by the month; by the quarter; and by the year. Most businesses have seasons of business where the seasons affect how much business they do. It is good to be aware of your slow season so that you can look for opportunities in those seasons that could bring your monthly revenues up and help you through those slower seasons.

You need to know the cost of doing business. You will have overheads that don't change, and you will have variable costs that do change, and that can be adjusted. To be competitive, you need to know your cost. You need to know your cost per item or your costs of services. Without knowing the cost, one could think they were busy and did okay, only to realize that because the costs were higher than the sale price of the item or service, your business was slowly sinking into extinction, if not corrected in time.

Obviously, most of us are in business to make a profit. Opportunities for profit must be in place to continue to grow the business. There are at least two aspects of profit that are important. One would be the profit level you desire for your business, and the other would be a profit level your consumers or clients will allow you to dictate in part by the competition. Without a reasonable amount of profit, your business will be challenged to grow, and you will be under constant stress. It is very possible your business will not survive. Profit is a good thing.

A balance sheet is also a must for any business seeking to grow and survive. The balance sheet will tell anyone who needs to know some relevant facts about the financial health of your business. This could be someone you are looking to for financing or investment.

The cash flow or working capital ratio will quickly give an understanding of how liquid or strong your business is, and how well it would survive an unexpected slowdown or an unexpected business expense. Ideally, you should work towards having the ability to withstand sudden change for three to six months. Less than that and your business could be in a tough situation if something threatening comes up.

The debt to equity ratio is another important ratio that your banker will keep an eye on. This will indicate borrowing strength. If your debt outpaces your equity you can be in an awkward position should something unexpected come up.

Your banker should be your friend. It is always a good practice to keep your bank account manager informed of what is going on in your business. If they are aware of what is happening, whether a challenge you are foreseeing or an opportunity, if they are walking with you through that experience, they will usually be more on your side should you need assistance of some sort. I have made it a practice to meet with our bankers at least annually, and ideally a couple of times a year.

There is an important aspect of finance I want you to consider. You may have been encouraged to sign personally for a bank loan. That means you are at risk of losing everything if there is a downturn in your business and you can't meet your obligations. Those that have your personal guarantee can swoop in and lay claim to anything or everything they need to satisfy your overdue loan. Most often they will sell these assets at auction price to cover the debt you owe. If that happens, it is very difficult to recover.

Ideally, you want to work towards limited guarantees. Negotiate a guarantee limited to that one piece of equipment, one property title, and not with an unlimited, 'take whatever what you need' guarantee. Too many well-intended borrowers have lost a lifetime of work due to this well-intended (by the borrower) guarantee. The thought often is, if they are willing to lend me the funds, I should be ready to guarantee payback. Very often the financier will look to cover themselves with as much of your assets as possible, ideally, all you have. Be very responsible in this important area of business finance responsibility.

In general, your management team should be growing in their understanding of the areas of financial concerns that they influence. By sharing pertinent information, their increased understanding will help them manage the areas of their responsibility and eventually they will enjoy the challenge of meeting the growth goals you agree to. Grow together, and when your team moves forward with you, with understanding, more and more opportunity will be available to you as the business owner to do what you enjoy most.

Developing a budget is critical to moving your team forward. A budgeted revenue and profit expectation to strive towards allows for creative thinking towards reaching the target. Budgeting expenditures increase expectations around staying within the agreed on goal and allows for discussions as to what is changing around that expectation. Cost increases can be better managed and then dealt with. There is a host of benefits around a working budget.

The old saying *'you cannot manage what you do not measure'* may be old, but the principle has not changed. In business, if you don't use good financial reporting methods you will be challenged to manage effectively. I say numbers tell stories if the figures are arranged in a manner that the story is easily told. Good reporting will allow you to ask good questions that will enable you to gain the clarity that leads to practical action. Without good reporting you will be operating in a fog, hoping that you will hit your target. Without a real target, you are aiming at nothing. Again, as an old saying goes, *'Aim at nothing and you are sure to hit it.'*

An excellent way to encourage continued excitement around setting and achieving goals is to celebrate when you meet or surpass them. The *'what's in it for me'* should have an interesting answer to your team. If it is all about you, that can be demotivating. If it is merely a measure to assure someone that they can expect to keep their job if targets are hit, that can be less than motivating. The greatest motivation is celebrating exceeded targets, shared with those who help meet or ideally exceed the targeted goals.

Everyone benefits when goals that are set are achieved, especially in the kingdom of God. The principles that are applied to business can be applied to the management of the church.

For example, setting goals for evangelism makes some people nervous. Some will fear that it will result in the manipulation of others into a *"decision"* for Christ just to increase numbers. Others may think the approach is too man-centered.

None of these concerns is legitimate. God alone saves. It is also true that we must be careful not to manipulate others into a false sense of spiritual security. It is also true that setting goals can lead to impersonal evangelism and a man-centered focus, but with God at the helm we, His team builders can manage the church to resemble the Kingdom of God. Goal setting can be used as effectively in the church, as in any business.

11
Stop Working Overtime. Start Having Some Fun

Ecclesiastes 5:18
"This is what I have observed to be good: that it is appropriate for a person to eat, to drink and to find satisfaction in their toilsome labor under the sun during the few days of life God has given them—for this is their lot."

Good employees are worth investing in. There are more and more people concerned that good employees will be more and harder to find in future years. If that is true, creating an environment where people can enjoy coming to work and have the desire to do their best should be an objective for any business owner serious about growing their business. Life at work should be productive and at the same time fun and meaningful. Good productivity, however, depends a lot on motivation. It has been proven that the worst jobs can be enjoyed if there is a good team spirit in place and the team enjoys working with each other. The work that they are called to do will get done and will get done efficiently.

Creating a fun environment takes energy, focus, and good intentions. There are whole seminars created on how to develop a workplace that is both fun and productive.

A program that rewards tenure is encouraging. Many companies recognize people every five years with 10, and 20 having a higher recognition. Your employees should feel appreciated and to recognize them for a job well done, and the time they invested with you, goes a long way.

A program that recognizes people for going the extra mile also builds motivation. Employees should have the ability to recognize each other as well as managers recognizing their staff. There are many different ways of rewarding people, and a well thought out reward plan will create even more fun, as employees go the extra mile. Always remember the question most employees will ask, *"What's in it for me?"* If we can provide an encouraging answer, everyone wins.

Add to your calendar events that become enjoyable; yearly social activities and opportunities for your team to stay in touch with each other. When the family at home supports and encourages your employee to continue at your place of business you have an even more dedicated and motivated employee. Thus, family events are important as well. Events where the children are recognized, where a spouse or significant other are included and appreciated are very important.

Another opportunity worth considering is programs where employees' dreams are recognized and where the company has a way of coming alongside that employee to see that dream come true. One can only imagine the excitement that would start to build throughout your team if their dreams were heard and ideas were thought up creatively to make dreams come true. This may seem somewhat out in the left field, but I am convinced from my experiences, that those that take this opportunity seriously will take their business to a new level of excitement and opportunity for everyone involved.

What about a scholarship program that awards your employees students? This program should be carefully thought out and award students that go above and beyond the call of duty. Such things could be considered as volunteer hours, good attitude and effort both at home, at school, and their part-time workplace. This could be a great opportunity to come alongside your employees and develop a program that, not only helps the child in due time but, gains appreciation and dedication from your employee and their child, and begins at an earlier age to build in that child characteristics that will benefit them for the rest of their life. Again, everybody wins, and you are not only building a stronger team at work, but you are building families for the future.

I firmly believe that our opportunity as business owners goes far beyond the business itself. Our opportunity goes far beyond just serving our clients and providing our employees a paycheck every two weeks. I believe a serious attempt should be sought out to come alongside our employees and benefit them physically, emotionally, mentally and spiritually.

We have an opportunity to bring wholesomeness to the individuals within our employment and their families and build our communities. We can make a much bigger difference with right vision and purpose than one may have ever dreamed possible. Please take this aspect of business ownership seriously, and you will be well rewarded for it.

Solomon understood the concept of *'fun.'* He lived his life in such a way that he denied himself no pleasure, and yet at the end of his days, he could say, **"Fear God. Keep His commandments" (Ecclesiastes 12:13).** The fact is, he both enjoyed himself and lived a rewarding life. Not to say that we are going to go the extreme that he did.

There is an old saying that I heard growing up, *"All work, and no play makes Jack a dull boy."* Believe it or not, we were created for pleasure. God desires that we have fun. Just look at the life of Jesus and His Disciples. I envision that there must have been much laughter as the power of God begun to set captives free. When the lame started to walk, they must have laughed with joy. Even King David understood the importance of having fun.

I firmly believe depression will visit those whose life is built around just work. If they don't make time for family, recreation, and fun, it can have a severe impact on the brain. Our ability to laugh and have fun suggest that it should be built into our lives. If we spend lots of time on our business, then there has to be time set apart for fun. Nothing boosts the morale of employees like having a day out with co-workers and family outside the confines of the business environment.

You need to recognize that there are just so many hours in a day. Overtime is built on the premise that there are things to be done today, that cannot wait until tomorrow. While this may be true to some extent, it is not always true. There is no purpose in driving yourself, and your business beyond what would be considered normal. The truth is, even if the need arises for overtime, those who commit to it should be adequately remunerated. Leave plenty of room for fun, leisure and family time.

12
Start Working "On" Your Business

Ecclesiastes 8:15
"So I commend the enjoyment of life, because there is nothing better for a person under the sun than to eat and drink and be glad. Then joy will accompany them in their toil all the days of the life God has given them under the sun."

Now that you have organized your business to a point where you are starting to enjoy it, your employees are starting to enjoy their work and their place in the business, and they are energized towards making a difference for everyone concerned, what do you do now? Now is the time to get serious about growing your opportunity. Now you can spend more time working on your business.

A mastermind group consists of people you respect, who will be honest with you to look at your business and ask you questions that others may not have the boldness to do so. The people you invite to this group are those you respect to brainstorm with you, to consider options with you, to ask tough questions of you, to hold you accountable to getting things done that you have committed to do, and through it all, to help you take your business to places you have never gone before. Your mastermind group ideally has a variety of strengths. You should have someone with the financial strength to ask you questions related to the financial health of your business and the matrix that will allow you to assess that health. You should have creative thinkers who help come up with new ideas to grow your opportunities. You should have people that have strength in human resources that ask you questions relating to your employees. You should have people who are strong in marketing and sales to ask you questions about the growth of your company whether you are still focused on the right markets, and whether you are tending to sales and the strategic plans that allow for continued growth. Collectively these people should hold you accountable for making sure that you get things done, that changes are made promptly, and that your company continues to serve its stakeholders and the community in which it exists.

The opportunity you have working with your mastermind group is to think outside the box. One might believe that a quiet getaway would allow for thinking outside the box. While it is true that quiet reflection might allow for coming up with new creative ideas, it is also true that you are the sum total of all your thoughts. So for a new train of thought to come in, you need to invite others into the opportunity to help you think outside the box.

Very often one idea offered up by someone will trigger an entirely new and supportive idea by another and through a brainstorming event, wonderful new un-thought of ideas will become new opportunities. Be sure to have creative thinkers on this team. The ideas can eventually be worked out by others, but this is where creative thinking happens. Have fun with it, and allow for every idea to be captured. No idea is a bad idea. Yes, it is true you can't take every idea and put it to work. You have to evaluate them, prioritize them, and then process them and eventually put them to work.

Investing in ongoing training for your management team, as well as any other employee that would like to improve their contribution to your business, and others around them is an excellent investment. I thoroughly believe that ongoing education with varying emphasis is good for everyone. There are many ways of doing this, from investing in a library of good reading material, short courses, in-house trainers, etc. This sends a message to your team that you value their contribution.

Have you considered the benefits of a coach? A business coach that walks with you in your business and encourages you to stay accountable to goals and objectives that you have set for your business and your personal life is a very effective way of moving your business forward and growing your abilities for both business and personal purposes. A coach is not the same as a consultant, but both have their place. You will at times need to bring in a consultant who specializes in the particular area of opportunity to assist you in bringing focus to an area of opportunity or challenge. A coach is ideally someone you have walking with you for a period of time. These may be different at times, but it has been proven over and over that most people will go farther in pursuit of excellence with accountability than without.

What is your vision for the company? Where do you see the opportunities? Where would you hope to take this company in the future if the possibilities continue to grow? If your current growth maintains itself, where would you be in five years? New facilities? Expanded facilities? New equipment? Is there a need for employees with different skills than you currently have on your team?

Every business has a vision. It is from this vision that long term and short term goals are derived. Goals and objectives point to vision, and what does the Bible say about vision?

Where there is no revelation, people cast off restraint; but blessed is the one who heeds wisdom's instruction. (Proverbs 29:18)

Start Working "On" Your Business

Are you beginning to see how the principles of the Bible can significantly aid in the success of your business? Yes, people have built a successful business without God, but not outside of the principles outlined in the Bible. In other words, you can use the principles, without submitting your heart to God, and still experience good results. What I have purported through this book, is not a separation, instead a syncing of our divine destiny, purpose and what we do. If we try to separate them, we make the journey all the more difficult.

Take the time to seek to envision what your company could look like in the future. Where you would like to take it, combined with demands for growth in service, may need considerable attention at some point. It is important to take the time to understand the vision for yourself, and to share the vision with your team. The vision for the future of your company starts with you. I encourage you to share your vision with those that you are looking to assist in leading your company.

If your team is on board with your vision, exciting times lie ahead for you. When you have taken the time to understand and agree on the vision for your company and the anticipated needs for that vision to be realized, it is important that you start to take time as well for the intermediate steps. Taking the time to plan the steps needed over the next one to five years will help ensure a smooth and exciting realization of the vision.

How about your team member's personal goals and dreams? Everyone should have a dream, something to strive after. We should all have reasons to look into the future toward something that will take time, planning, hopes, and a variety of other needs that are not instantly available. It is a healthy place to be. The dream could be a few months away, or maybe a year and hundreds or thousands of dollars away, but whatever the dream is, it should be something that one cannot achieve in a short space of time. Looking forward to something that stretches us, keeps us in the game. There is something about sharing your dream and having others come alongside to support us in achieving that dream that is beneficial both for the dreamer and the one supporting the dreamer.

In your case, if you can be the supporter of the dream, that is a stretch away from reality for one of your team members. If you come alongside them to help them achieve that dream, everyone wins.

Take the time to know your team's dreams. Be an active participant in what they want to achieve for themselves, and they will go above and beyond to ensure that your vision for your business will be realized.

Too many business owners treat their employees as liabilities. Even if at times this is true, it should not be used as ammunition against them. I have heard people tell their workers how others are lined up for their position. This de-values your employees and reduces them to nothing but a replaceable battery.

The challenge is always to put the business above the persons, because in some sense, we make a separation. What is more important, the body, or the members of the body; a building, or the occupants; your business, or the employees? The company is only as good as the team we employ. They are important and valuable as they are the ones who will help us drive the business forward.

13

Doing Business From A Kingdom Perspective

As business minded Christians, we must ask ourselves very poignant questions as it relates to going into business. One of the most important to ask is, *"Why should Christians go into business?"* I would assume that one possible answer would be to provide goods and services that are depicting the qualities of God's children. The goal of business and that of ministry is very different. The primary purpose of ministry is to save souls for heaven and in so doing all the miseries of the wealthy and poor will dissipate.

But what if both can be combined? What if your business, could also be your ministry? After all, that is where you spend a whole lot of time, and energy, right?

Some may see business as just a way out. For those who say the purpose of business is to save themselves from poverty, I profess that God is the answer to that and Jesus is the way, the Truth, and the Light. The purpose of Kingdom business entrepreneurs goes far beyond just establishing a 'cash cow.'

"The Spirit of the Lord is on me, because he has anointed me to proclaim good news to the poor. He has sent me to proclaim freedom for the prisoners and recovery of sight for the blind, to set the oppressed free, to proclaim the year of the Lord's favor." (Luke 4:18-19).

As Christian business team leaders, we serve the interest of the whole person because the Kingdom of God perspective focuses on the entire human being: physical, spiritual, social, mental, and emotional. The person is comprehensive. The solution to humanity's need must be holistic. While those of the world tend to focus on meeting the physical needs of their internal and external customers, catering to the whole individual is a recipe for success.

We are co-laborers with God, and business is part of our calling and what gives us meaning in life. So how are Christian business owners to think about their business? If leading as a Christian does not mean going to work, setting up our soap box and giving a weekly sermon, how do we conduct ourselves? Christians should make others want to know more about God, and one way to spark interest is how we conduct ourselves as business people. They should want to emulate us and our way of life. What should minister for us is our lives. We are an epistle to those who may not readily take up their Bibles and read it. Just as Jesus says, **"If you have seen me, you have seen**

the Father" (John 14:9). We too need to reflect Christ, so those who see us, see Him.

Kingdom business is a movement spreading globally—because it is God's movement, not born of man but of the *'I Am.'* In this age, we have more people becoming Entrepreneurs than any other time in the history of humanity. As a matter of fact, they now include entrepreneurship as a part of the school curriculum. Our University's spew out thousands of graduates every year, with only a small percentage of them acquiring employment in the area of study. We need more businesses, and this is an opportunity for those in Christ to begin to take these high places within our society, from which we can cause a paradigm shift.

We know that the Kingdom of God will invade every area and eventually take over every realm. Business is one of the seven mountains that the Kingdom of God needs to possess. It is described in Luke 13:18 as a growing tree that gradually fills the whole earth until all the birds can nest in its branches. Those of us who are called to Kingdom business are a unique breed of people. Our thrill does not come from aspects of the church alone. Rather, we are driven to succeed and make money, to expand and branch out in our communities with services and products that exemplify God. Kingdom business people are not particularly motivated by a personal desire for money but find ourselves motivated to establish a new economy and set a precedent for a new way of life. The success we seek is more to see His Kingdom established in the business realm.

Ideally, we strive for our businesses to reflect the Kingdom of God. So we endeavor to make our employees work in jobs they love doing. This may seem revolutionary, but there is another reason for working other than the drudgery of having to earn a living to scrape by. We have been so long in the confines of this dying age that it's hard for our minds to grasp an economy where business and labor takes place out of the joy of providing it. This is life when His Kingdom is established, and businesses will flourish without greed involved.

In a Kingdom company, there will be an understanding that all men are equal, without regard to race, creed, or social status. As Paul points out in Galatians 3:28; there is neither Jew nor Greek, male nor female, but all are one in Christ. Business owners will weigh matters based on a person's abilities for a task. They will appreciate all faithful workers in their business and not use or manipulate one another for their gain. They should strive to hire workers that embrace the values and culture of the business. It may seem surprising to know, but God pays careful attention to how we conduct our businesses.

Now listen, you rich people, weep and wail because of the misery that is coming on you.[2] **Your wealth has**

rotted, and moths have eaten your clothes.³ Your gold and silver are corroded. Their corrosion will testify against you and eat your flesh like fire. You have hoarded wealth in the last days.⁴ Look! The wages you failed to pay the workers who mowed your fields are crying out against you. The cries of the harvesters have reached the ears of the Lord Almighty. (James 5:1-4)

Hear this, you who trample the needy and do away with the poor of the land, saying, "When will the New Moon be over that we may sell grain, and the Sabbath be ended that we may market wheat?"— skimping on the measure, boosting the price and cheating with dishonest scales, buying the poor with silver and the needy for a pair of sandals, selling even the sweepings with the wheat. The Lord has sworn by himself, the Pride of Jacob: "I will never forget anything they have done. (Amos 8:4-7).

God judges our attitude to business as part of our personal relationship with Him. In Malachi 3:1, He vows to avenge the laborers who have been oppressed by poor business practice, and we may well be living in that time right now. Therefore, all dealings should be conducted openly for His inspection and business owners can sleep at night knowing this.

When Trouble Comes

In December 2005, just a couple days before Christmas, a friend of mine drove into the yard. I had not seen him in a while, and it was closing the end of the day at work, and quiet enough to stop and have a coffee. I asked the usual question *"How are you doing, Jack"?* As usual, his response with a smile was, *'Life is good.'* I said, *"Great"!* His smile and confirmation that all was well may have ordinarily ended that part of the conversation. His smile and cheerful greeting made me wonder if the challenge I had been aware of was behind him. He had been going through a tough challenge in his business for some years. His business had been audited by CRA resulting in a very unfair assessment. This wasn't just unjust in his estimation; it had also been deemed extremely unjust by both professional accountants and tax lawyers. He had been trying to resolve this issue for some years.

The last time I had seen him, it had still not been resolved. Thus, the answer *'great'* wasn't satisfactory to me. I asked him if he had made any progress in having this dispute resolved. His smile disappeared, and he responded that no, the dispute was still not resolved. My friend, with his team of professionals, was still looking for a solution.

I looked at him quietly and tried to understand the frustration he was going through. My experience was different, and I could handle it, but I didn't think that I would be as resolved to calmly continue this fight he had if his were mine. I suggested to him that there had to be a way that he could legally address this issue and put it behind him. He agreed. *"However"* he said, *"if I proceed to bring this to a close on my own, after all these years that I have been telling people that God would see me through this and that my financial accounting procedures would be justified, the message I would now be telling people is that I no longer believe God can see me through this after all."* That was a very profound response for me.

We had been going through a tough period in our own business. By this time, it had been a six-year financial struggle. Month to month I wasn't sure we would survive, and I often wondered how long we could continue. It was like going broke every month; our small ship almost sinking, but not entirely. We were just barely hanging on, never getting ahead of the curve, and scrambling each and every month.

We had lost a live poultry transport contract in 1999 that had provided over 50% of our revenues up until that time, and we weren't ready for that loss of income. We did not see it coming. We thought that after 18 years of continuous service, the equipment update we had been talking about with the processing plant for a few years would be a new opportunity for us. We had made preparations for it; looking at various changes we would need to anticipate, the different types of equipment to complete the package, the financing needs, changes in employee training, etc. One thing we were too sure of, was that we would undoubtedly continue to provide the live haul service. This was a gross mistake and nearly took our company down.

We had six months' notice, not nearly enough to prepare us. A large part of our equipment was now obsolete. Instead of training people for a newly updated service, we were laying off staff. I made some decisions during that initial period, one being that I would do all I could to survive this challenge, and keep as many of our team of employees together as possible. That meant growing the other business services we had. That decision, resulting in more equipment, more staff, a sales team, causing extremely tight cash flow, resulted in 10 very challenging years before we began to breathe a sigh of relief.

At this point, when my friend dropped by, we were about half way through our journey. Truthfully, I had no idea where we were on this journey. I was wondering if we would survive. I was beginning to think it was the end. I had considered my options, how I could get out of it all. If I could have given up easily without consequence, I would have.

However, that day, when he shared with me his quiet confidence that he firmly believed and trusted that God would see him successfully through his difficulty;

my friend believed that God would see me through my challenge, if I trusted Him to, if I had the courage to put my faith in Him. A new understanding of what I was going through opened up to me. I too was on a journey. I didn't know how long, but gradually there was a new dawning, an awakening, and a new found confidence that I did not have to fear, and I certainly didn't have to travel this journey alone. In fact, I was never on the journey alone. I was in the firm, loving grip of the Master and had the option of trusting Him to take me through to a new day, a better day. He had a Master plan, and He would see me through.

I now believe that God's love doesn't keep us from challenges in life, but He promises to walk with us through them and to show Himself strong on our behalf in the midst of them. I learned that day that I needed to surrender my challenges to His care, and that He would see me through, and that there would be a better day. This confidence is what is referred to in Hebrews as *'Faith.'*

I believe there are challenges in our lives that we are to face that He entrusts to us. He gives us the capacity to bear up under the pressures of whatever problem we may be facing for the purpose of showing those that are looking on that He can take us through. Ultimately it's not our strength and not our capacity that allows us to bear up under the strain of whatever we may be facing. It's His.

Some of you may be facing relationship challenge, health challenge, financial challenge, loss of a loved one, and more. There are some challenges that we face in life, some more than others. There's no escaping the fact that you will face challenges. The question is, how will you face it? Will you go forward in your strength, determined to take on the challenge, face what comes? Will you surrender or are you determined to win? Will you give it your all, or go down fighting, even if it *'kills you'*. You can be the hero in your story.

Maybe you are about to cave in. You are just about done, and ready to give up. You have given it your all, and you fought hard, carried your load all the way and no one can say you gave up easily. You may be breathless, exhausted, spent, worn out, and done. I believe there's another way. Trust Him. I believe that is what He is asking you to do right now. Go forward believing in Him, trusting in Him to take you through this journey of the challenge to a better day.

In time, you will be that person who walks with someone going through a season of challenge, who can look to you for encouragement and support through their storm, because you would have been there before them.

Many challenges face Christians and non-Christians at different aspects of our journey here on earth. We can draw on the faithfulness of two women in the Bible who overcame their emotional and financial challenges to pull through.

Each woman bore a heavy burden of grief. Naomi had been a widow for years, but she was mourning more recent losses—the deaths of her two sons, Chilion and Mahlon. Ruth too was grieving. Mahlon was her husband. She and Naomi were heading to the same destination, the town of Bethlehem in Israel. In a way, though, their journeys differed. Naomi was going home. Ruth was venturing into the unknown, leaving her kin, her homeland, and all its customs, including its gods, behind her. (See Ruth 1:3-6).

Ruth was young, and she was making a drastic change. She was becoming a refugee to make a new life for herself and to take care of Naomi, but showed loyalty and insisted on staying with Naomi who was about to face incredible hardships.

Ruth said:

Where you go, I will go, and where you stay I will stay. Your people will be my people and your God my God. Where you die, I will die, and there I will be buried. (Ruth 1:16b-17a)

Ruth worked in a field gleaming with the men. What she made was barely enough to buy food. However, in time, her faith would see her through to a day of rejoicing. She too was taken through her challenges to a better day.

In 1 Peter 4:12-13 it says, **Dear friends, do not be surprised at the fiery ordeal that has come on you to test you, as though something strange were happening to you. But rejoice inasmuch as you participate in the sufferings of Christ, so that you may be overjoyed when his glory is revealed.**

In 2 Corinthians 4:8-11 it says, **"We are hard pressed on every side, but not crushed; perplexed, but not in despair; persecuted, but not abandoned; struck down, but not destroyed. We always carry around in our body the death of Jesus, so that the life of Jesus may also be revealed in our body. For we who are alive are always being given over to death for Jesus' sake, so that his life may also be revealed in our mortal body."**

We will always be facing challenges, as our spirits are being refined into something finer than gold. We are all overcomers in our faith.

For I the Lord thy God will hold thy right hand, saying unto thee, Fear not; I will help thee (Isaiah 41:13). He is our deliverer in a time of need. Even though it is our test, we are not left to suffer alone; that is when God is carrying us.

Life is always full of challenges. Just when we think that everything is going smoothly and according to God's plan, we are faced with a challenge, something that causes us to feel inadequate once again, something that causes us to seek His direction and strength.

What a challenge it must have been for Jesus to die. When the Last Supper was ended, Jesus went to the Garden of Gethsemane for a quiet place to pray. He knew what was about to happen. He knew Judas was at that very moment plotting to betray him.

Jesus could have run. It is impossible for any of us even to begin to imagine the weight that was on Jesus' shoulders. He knew what He must do. And even though He implored God in all earnestness for deliverance from the ordeal of crucifixion, He completely yielded His personal will to God's divine plan.

We are called to be like Jesus and stand firm through our challenges and bear our trials and crosses as we help our Father with His divine plan.

Consider it pure joy, my brothers and sisters, whenever you face trials of many kinds, because you know that the testing of your faith produces perseverance. Let perseverance finish its work so that you may be mature and complete, not lacking anything. If any of you lacks wisdom, you should ask God, who gives generously to all without finding fault, and it will be given to you. (James 1:2-5).

We are here to fulfill our Father's mission of establishing His Kingdom here on earth. As business people, we are in a lofty position to transform this world, one person at a time.

Epilogue

We now come to the conclusion of this little book. I want to thank you for patiently hearing my story and hopefully noticing the immense joy that I have experienced and continue to experience being a follower of Christ in business.

The joy of this journey started with a question that was asked of a group of Christian business owners gathered at a conference some years ago. The speaker pointed us to the Scripture reference that tells us that we all will give an account before God one day of how we have lived our lives. The speaker asked us what it might be that God would hold us accountable for as business owners. Might He ask us how many employees we employed, how many buildings we had built, how many businesses we had run, how many cities we had been engaged in, how many dollars we had given to mission projects, and we can only imagine how many related questions and topics of discussion we as business owners feel quite good about. Or, he asked, may God quite simply only ask us this one question, *"What did you do with all the people I sent to you?"*

That question was burnt into my heart and mind that day and has never left. In a good way, I continue to search for an answer on how to engage with that question successfully. To have a reply, should that be a question God would ask me on judgment day.

I can say today; that question has given me immense joy in my journey. I realize that enjoying business is more about enjoying the people that I journey this life with. It is a wonderful place to interact with employees, clients, and vendors, and hopefully, enrich those lives.

Thus, I pose the same question to you, as you continue to make a difference in the lives of others. May God bless you richly to enjoy that which He has given you, and to manage it to His glory.

References

http://ceo-book.com/business-operates-gods-economy/

http://www.kingdombusinessconnection.com/spiritual-principles/how-business-operates-in-gods-economy/

http://kingdombuildersbusiness.wordpress.com/

http://ceo-book.com/tag/bible/

http://ceo-book.com/tag/service/

http://www.kga.org.za/wp/wp-content/uploads/2015/11/How-Business-Operates-in-Gods-Economy.pdf

www.ingramcontent.com/pod-product-compliance
Lightning Source LLC
Chambersburg PA
CBHW070247190526
45169CB00001B/326